York Today

The Dean's Park

MONK BAR

York Minster

St William's College

Merchant Taylors' Hall

HIGH PETERGATE

STONEGATE

LOW PETERGATE

St Anthony's Hall

COLLIERGATE

Guildhall

THE SHAMBLES

St Sampson's Square (formerly Thursday Market)

St Crux Hall

CONEY STREET

PAVEMENT

FOSSGATE

All Saints Pavement

RIVER FOSS

FOSS BRIDGE

OUSE BRIDGE

Merchant Adventurers' Hall

WALMGATE

KING'S STAITH

Clifford's Tower

Castle Site

Baile Hill

WALMGATE BAR

0   500
feet

N

The York Merchant Adventurers
and their Hall

The York Merchant Adventurers
and their Hall

Edited by **Pamela Hartshorne**

THIRD MILLENNIUM
PUBLISHING, LONDON

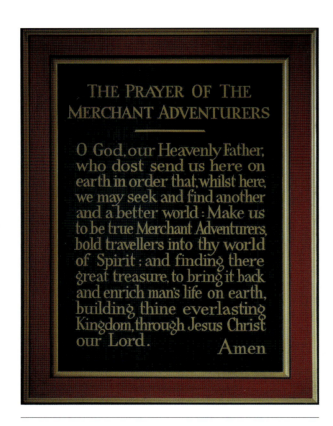

THE PRAYER OF THE
MERCHANT ADVENTURERS
———
O God, our Heavenly Father,
who dost send us here on
earth in order that, whilst here,
we may seek and find another
and a better world : Make us
to be true Merchant Adventurers,
bold travellers into thy world
of Spirit : and finding there
great treasure, to bring it back
and enrich man's life on earth,
building thine everlasting
Kingdom, through Jesus Christ
our Lord.   Amen

Previous page: *The intricately carved bargeboards on the Hall's north-west façade date from the late 16th or early 17th century.*

EDITOR'S NOTE

Although I often admired the Hall as I walked past it, until I began work on this book I had no idea just how rich a history lay behind this wonderful building. It has been a privilege to get to know the story of the Hall and of the people who have cared for it over more than 650 years and I am very grateful indeed to Paul Shepherd and to the other members of the Working Group who gave so much of their time and expertise to this book: Peter Addyman, Darrell Buttery, James Finlay, Rita Freedman, Kate Giles, Jill Redford, Michael Saville and Richard Shephard.

A project of this kind depends on the generosity and help of many people. I owe particular thanks to James Finlay and Lauren Marshall for their unflagging patience and support, and to Jill Redford for guiding me through the Company archives. I am especially grateful, too, to Kate Giles for sharing her expert knowledge of the archaeology of the Hall, and to David Palliser for taking the time to read and comment on the history chapters.

I would also like to take the opportunity to thank the following people: Louise Wheatley, Kath Webb, Peter Young at the York Minster archive, the Stained Glass Trust, Fiona Diaper at the Quilt Museum, Agnes Winter, Christine Hemingbrough and Mike Andrews at the York Archaeological Trust.

Finally, it was a pleasure, as always, to work with photographer Kippa Matthews, and with Matt Wilson, who designed this book.

Pamela Hartshorne

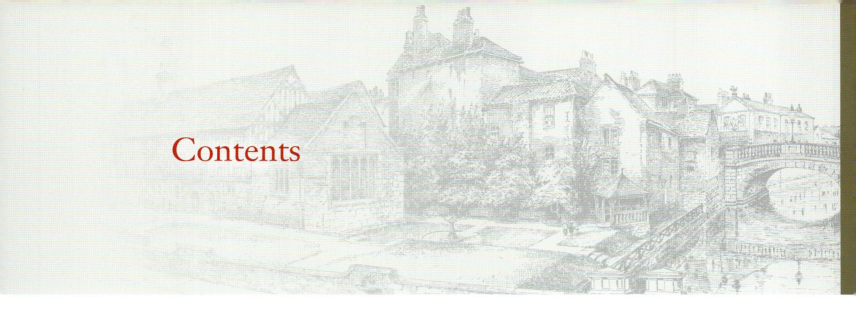

Contents

A new Company history

by Paul Shepherd (Governor 2009–10)

The Company of Merchant Adventurers of the City of York has long wished to have a record of its history and Hall. This was discussed at successive meetings of the Court of Assistants between September 2009 and February 2010 when it was decided to proceed with a history, subject to raising the necessary funding from Company members and other outside organisations.

No member was more supportive of this than Michael Hollingbery, who raised the idea at a members' luncheon in May 2009, the last Company event that he attended. Sadly he died six months later but left, without any pre-conditions, a very generous legacy. In view of his earlier comments it seemed very appropriate to transfer a significant part of this legacy to the funding of a new Company history. After consultation, his widow, Karen, confirmed her willingness for Michael's legacy to be used for this purpose and this was later unanimously supported by the Court.

Thanks also to the generosity of many members, individuals and particularly the Noel Terry Trust, the necessary figure was reached in less than three months. A list of donors is included in the appendix.

The Court was very clear that this book should be a serious and properly researched history of the Company with more about the past than the present. Every effort has been made to fulfil this condition. It has been written by a team consisting of Company members with appropriate knowledge and experience of the Company, as well as academics and other specialists.

The book charts the progress of the Company through nearly seven centuries as it struggled to adapt to constantly changing times. Throughout its life, the common factor binding the membership has been the Hall. Almost certainly the finest medieval building of its type in the world, it has provided a place for the Company to conduct its business. Today the building is in excellent condition, is in daily use and visited by over 20,000 people every year. However, it has not always been so and it has required the commitment

The arms of the Merchant Adventurers of England, used by the Company until 1969, above the Fossgate entrance to the Hall.

and efforts of members for over 650 years to bring the building to the present condition. As you will read, it has been an eventful journey from the 14th to the 21st century, during which the Company has regularly had to adjust to ever-changing circumstances.

Without question the prime role of the Company today is the maintenance of the Hall and Chapel. However, the Company must be about more than the preservation of the building, and its role in the 21st century has been deeply considered. Clearly this will be very different from its origins. The Statement of Core Purposes below has been recently

agreed by the Court and sets out how that role is perceived today.

- To maintain and improve the Hall for the education and enjoyment of the public and as an important place of business.
- To be an active force in the economic development of the City of York and the surrounding region.
- To seek to identify, encourage and inspire young entrepreneurs in York and the surrounding area.
- To provide mutual benefit, support and friendship to fellow members of the Company.
- To fulfil the charitable objectives of the Company through the support of its members.
- To continue to uphold the Christian tradition of the Company whilst remaining open to all faiths and none.

The next challenge to which the members are fully committed is to implement the above and make a significant contribution to York and the surrounding region.

I hope that you enjoy reading this book and that it will, perhaps, help to inspire a new generation of entrepreneurs. In conclusion, and on behalf of all members of the Company, I wish you 'Bonne Aventure'.

Above: *The Charter Day Court is held annually.*

Right: *The trees along Piccadilly provide welcome shade in the summer.*

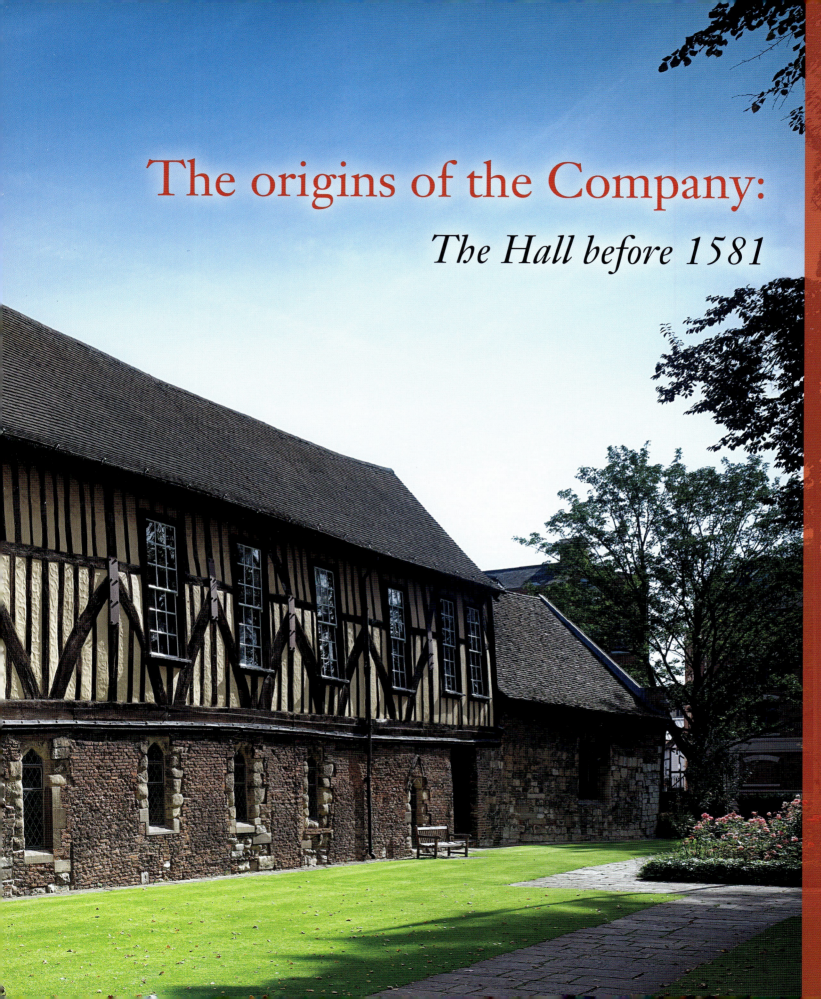

The origins of the Company:

The Hall before 1581

The origins of the Company:
The Hall before 1581

Some time in 1356, John Freboys, John Crome and Robert Smeton, citizens and merchants of York, spat on their palms and shook hands to seal a deal made with Sir William Percy. The agreement was formalised in December 1356 with a deed still in possession of the Company. In it, Sir William granted 'all that piece of ground with the buildings … in Fossgate' where the Hall now stands. The site was prone to flooding, and Percy may indeed have been glad to get rid of it, but there was a stone building of some status with its own chapel; and the location, next to Foss Bridge, the base of York's saltwater trade, and in the heart of the city's mercantile district, made it ideal for the merchants' purposes. All parties must have been well satisfied with the deal, which marked the start of an unbroken association between the Hall and the merchants of York that has lasted more than 650 years. Although the Company of Merchant Adventurers of the City of York did not exist in its present form until 1581, it has its origins in the deal that was struck that day in 1356.

What kind of place was York when the Hall was built? Strategically sited on the road north, it had played an important role in the wars with Scotland earlier in the 14th century. As late as 1319 the Scots invaders had come 'evene to York walles' and 'brent the subarbes', but as the Crown's attention turned increasingly to France, York played a less significant role in national affairs. Nonetheless, it remained the religious, administrative, social and economic centre of the North, and could still claim its historic position as England's 'second city'. It owed its prosperity to its position at the centre of a network of roads and rivers. Bulky items were most easily transported by water. Situated as it is at the confluence of the Ouse and the Foss, York had access to a

Previous pages: *Built in the mid-14th century, the Merchant Adventurers' Hall is one of the finest surviving semi-timbered medieval guild halls in the world.*

Above: *Charter issued by Sir Percy William granting land in Fossgate to John Freboys, John Crome and Robert Smeton; dated 16 December 1356.*

Left: *Sir William Percy's seal.*

wide hinterland served by the two rivers and those that drained into them, particularly the Derwent, Swale, Ure and Wharfe. The Ouse itself was still tidal as far as eight miles above the city, and the ships tied up at the quays on either side of the river linked York to Hull and thence to the great overseas markets in the Low Countries. It was, as Maud Sellers (*see box, p.70*) pointed out, 'an industrial asset of far-reaching importance'. Certainly the river traffic between York and Hull was vital to the merchants of York, and a source of concern and the subject of regulation well into the 19th century. Sacks of wool and grain, bales of cloth, and fothers of lead were loaded onto the ships at the busy quays, while wine, wax, oil, salt, dyestuffs, glass, copper and the spices that were so important in cooking were unloaded. Ginger and cloves, cinnamon and saffron, pepper and oranges all found their way from Africa, India and the Spice Islands to the staiths at York.

Less exotic goods were also traded in the city, which was the greatest market of the north. Corn, barley and pease were sold in the market on Pavement, poultry, game, meat, butter, cheese and eggs in Thursday Market. In York you could buy a pair of gloves or rushes for the hall floor, a lemon or a pewter dish, a horse or a book. People came to plead their cases in court, to visit the shrine of St William, to find work, to trade, to meet people, to gossip, and generally to do business. It was a bustling, vibrant city, dominated by the great stone bulks of the Minster and St Mary's Abbey on one side, and the two castles flanking the Ouse at the other.

View of Old Ouse Bridge by Edward Dayes (c.1801). Goods from all over the world were unloaded at the staiths in York until well into the 19th century.

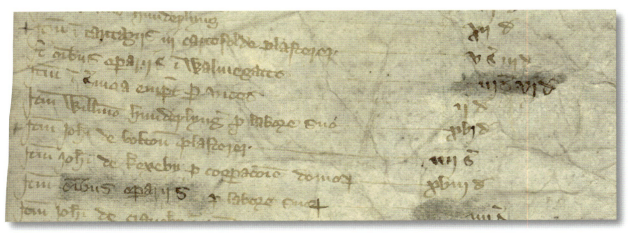

Left: *Detail of account roll dating from 1366–7. This extract begins: 'For carrying 3 cartloads of plaster 5s. 3d.; For all those working in Walmegatte 3s. 4d.; For occasional services 2d.; To William Hunderlyng for his work' 16d.'*

Below: *Panorama of York as it might have looked in the 15th century, by Edwin Ridsdale Tate (1915).*

The medieval city is often imagined as a squalid and chaotic place, but there was, in fact, a very clear system of administration and environmental regulation controlled by a council of aldermen. Participation in civic government was restricted to freemen, those who had inherited, earned or bought the freedom of the city. To be made free, a man had to show that he was capable of earning a living in a trade, usually by completing an apprenticeship, that he was responsible enough to play his part in civic life, and that his morals were sound enough to qualify him as one of the 'bons gens'. Freedom also enabled him to carry on a trade or a craft as a master. There may have been as many as 80 specialist crafts and trades in York during the medieval period, from butchers, bakers, masons and tailors to pinners, spurriers, cardmakers and scriveners. To practise a craft, a master had to be both a freeman and a member of the craft mystery, as guilds were referred to by contemporaries. Interestingly, there was no official mystery of mercers recorded until 1420, although there seems little doubt that merchants and mercers would have banded together for mutual benefit before that date.

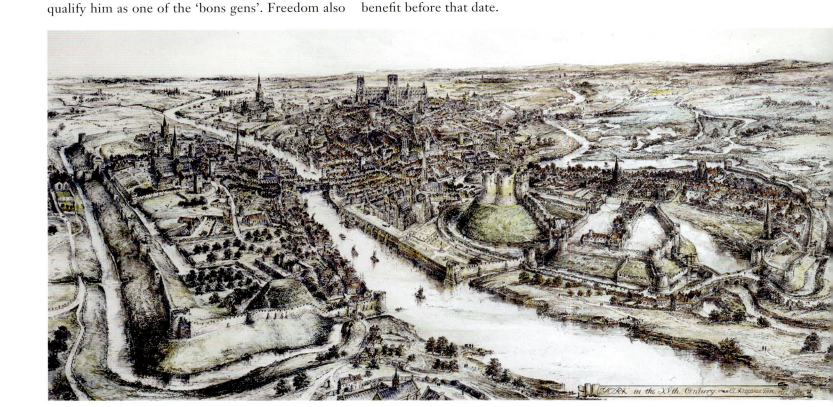

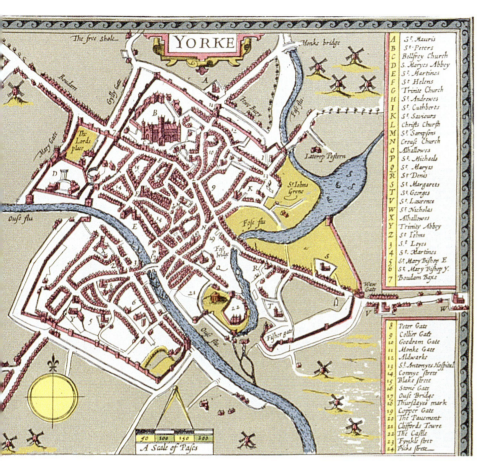

Life and work in 14th-century York were inextricably bound up with the Christian faith. There were at least 40 parish churches in the city, most within the walls, as well as the Minster, St Mary's Abbey and a number of friaries. Faith in late-medieval England was underpinned by a belief in the power of prayer and in the relationship between the living and the dead. After death, a Christian soul passed to Purgatory, where it was condemned to suffer before ascending to Heaven at last. That suffering, however, could be shortened by the prayers of the living. Wealthy individuals founded chantries and endowed priests to say masses on their behalf after their death, or purchased indulgences from the Church that took a certain number of years off the time their soul had to stay in Purgatory. Those without the money to endow their own chantries often chose to pool their resources and to form religious guilds or fraternities. A fraternity was founded on the belief that members could intercede for their dead 'brothers' and 'sisters' to lessen their suffering in Purgatory. They attended funerals and masses, lit candles, and prayed for the departed, in the knowledge that the same would be done for them in their turn. In life, too, members of the fraternity pledged to support each other. The friendship network was reinforced by feasts shared by all members, and provided a sense of communal identity that endured into the afterlife. Guilds had a devotional focus – often an altar, light or image within a parish church – and usually a charitable one as well, perhaps support for a *maison dieu* or a hospital offering shelter and care for the less fortunate.

13

John Freboys was a member of one such association based in St Crux Church on the Pavement. The acquisition of the land in Fossgate seems to have been a preliminary step in the founding of a fraternity in honour of Our Lord Jesus Christ and the Blessed Virgin Mary, and the speed with which building work started on the site to build a hall suggests that the membership had a very clear idea of what they wanted to achieve. The Hall, with its Chapel, its hospital offering succour to the poor, and the Great Hall where members could meet to discuss fraternity business and eat together, brought the three-pronged aims of the guild under one roof. Fraternity, charity and religion have underpinned the associations of those who used the Hall ever since, and continue to this day.

The Fraternity of Our Lord Jesus Christ and the Blessed Virgin Mary

Once the land was acquired, John Freboys and 12 other men applied to Edward III for a formal licence. Granted in March 1357, the licence gave them permission to found a guild for men and women in honour of Our Lord Jesus Christ and the Blessed Virgin Mary. The terms of the licence provided for a Master to be elected annually. The Master was to have custody of all the fraternity's property and possessions, and to enforce rules that had been agreed by all the members. Importantly, the licence enabled the guild to hold lands and rents up to an annual value of £10, revenue from which would provide for chaplains to celebrate divine service daily and pray for the well-being of all the members, the King and his family, and all the guild's benefactors, as well as for their souls after death.

The rents were also to be used for pious works, and the fraternity clearly had a hospital in mind. Medieval hospitals were religious institutions that offered spiritual and physical comfort to the poor and the infirm. Although many of the inmates were in practice sick or disabled, a hospital's primary purpose was spiritual rather than medical. It was staffed by chaplains, employed to provide prayers and commemoration for the founders, and assisted by lay men and women, who helped care for the unfortunate. A licence to found the hospital in the Undercroft of the Hall was not granted until 1371,

but it seems likely that it was planned from the outset as a very visible demonstration of the fraternity's charity. Henry Blyth, who died in 1365, left 20s. *ad fabricam et reparacionem novi hospitalis*.

John Freboys, who had been instrumental in acquiring the land from Sir William Percy, was the first Master of the fraternity. In an echo of Christ and the Apostles, the foundation deed names a further 12 men. Although four of them were merchants or mercers like Freboys, the fraternity was in no sense a trade association at this stage. Richard Thoresby, whose name also appears on the foundation deed, was a hosier, John Morby a potter and John Best a tanner. A draper, a spicer and a dyer were also listed.

A remarkable series of documents survive from the fraternity's early years. As well as the licences to found the guild, and later the hospital, the Company still holds account rolls for five years between 1357 and 1367 and a paper account book from 1358–69 which provide a vivid picture of the fraternity's activities. Members paid an entrance fee on joining the fraternity, and thereafter quarterly payments towards the various activities of the guild. It is likely that, as with other religious guilds, new members took an oath

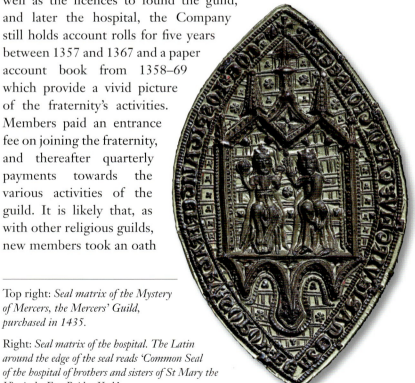

Top right: *Seal matrix of the Mystery of Mercers, the Mercers' Guild, purchased in 1435.*

Right: *Seal matrix of the hospital. The Latin around the edge of the seal reads 'Common Seal of the hospital of brothers and sisters of St Mary the Virgin by Foss Bridge York'.*

of initiation in which they promised to support each other in times of trouble and settle any disputes with fellow members within the fellowship. They were to keep the affairs of the fraternity to themselves and to attend the annual feast and the meetings that were held during the year to discuss business. Most importantly, the brothers and sisters had a duty to attend the funerals of their fellow members and provide masses for their souls. When Beatrice of Ampleforth died in 1368, a beadle was paid 2d. to summon members to her funeral, and the fraternity provided candles to burn around her body. Beatrice left 10s. to the fraternity in her will.

There is plenty of evidence of happier occasions in the account rolls too: meetings, entertaining, a feast for their brothers and sisters from Whitby. The fraternity acquired property in Walmgate, Castlegate, Fishergate and elsewhere, rents from which were put towards building the Hall. These houses had to be maintained, and there was soon an administrative team in place. By 1366 chamberlains, clerks, a beadle, an

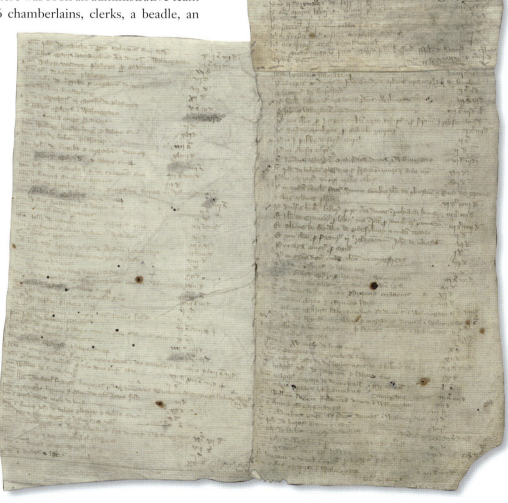

Account roll dating from 1366–7.

MERCHANTS' LETTERS

A collection of some 200 letters in the archive brings to life the realities of the merchants' trading operations. The papers date from *c.*1478–1647 and cover all aspects of trade. The struggles, trials and tribulations of the local merchants are well detailed in the papers. Competition was fierce and the rules were not always enforced. Local merchants were frequently at a disadvantage in comparison with the London and even the foreign traders.

The activities of the Easterlings, as merchants from the cities that made up the Hanseatic League were known, particularly exercised the northern merchants in the late 15th century and a draft petition to Edward IV voiced their complaints. The foreign traders were coming over to the North where they got away with grossly unfair practices. 'Thay brynge thare schippys to all the havyns, crykkes, and vyllages, … and they goo to all farys and markettes, and to any towne and vyllage … to the gryett hurtt, damage, and loosse to the foresayd marchauntes.' The foreigners were trading all sorts of commodities, 'wellvetts, sattans, damaskes, Holland clootte, and other marchandays, wych is no part of thayre commodyte, perrper, saffron, clovs, and maase, with all other grossere, and allso all manner of wynys and pottre wayre'. They took ready money and 'kepys all the goold and syllver and beste payment that they may gett', and did not reciprocate trade by buying locally. Conversely the activities of the English merchants abroad were very restricted. They were not allowed to conduct their trade abroad except with a freeman. Non-freemen were forbidden to sell to the English merchants.

Another petition in 1478 sets out articles of complaint by the merchants of York, Hull, Beverley, Scarborough, Whitby and other places in the North against John Pickering, the governor of the merchants' colony abroad, appointed by the London merchants. He was accused of keeping the contributions made by the northern towns to maintain their own governor to safeguard northern interests. Pickering blatantly desired to diminish northern trade. He used his influence to get the toll collectors in Brabant to exact double taxes upon northern men and to distrain their goods if they refused. He raised the trading fees of the northern masters and apprentices and forced them to show their cloth in places 'inconvenyent and not profitable'. Fortunately Pickering was unpopular even with the London merchants and was summoned to their court and appeared 'hawty and roiall'. He was forced to beseech forgiveness. The episode cost the York mercers both trouble and money. The Earl of Northumberland and the Duke of Gloucester (later Richard III, who was close to the City of York) probably intervened on their behalf.

A century later there was a petition asking the Merchants Adventurers of England to request a hearing in the Queen's Council asking for fair and reciprocal trade. The Dutch merchants had 20 times the Merchants' number of ships of 200 tons or above in 1572. They had built 'fluitships' with flat bottoms able to carry bulky goods more cheaply, particularly timber from Scandinavia and the Baltic. English clothiers tried to use Dutch ships to carry their goods, and importers of timber and grain found the same advantage, causing petitions from English companies to Crown and Parliament to ban foreign ships from carrying goods to and from England. These went unheeded for some considerable time as both James I and Charles I did not call parliament for years on end. Wars added to the difficulties and during the last quarter of the 16th century and most of the 17th, many European nations were at war with one or other of their neighbours. Armed men-of-war transported armies overseas and many a merchantman fell victim to their depredations. This was also the age of the privateer, 'the King's left arm by the sea', authorised to seize and plunder vessels. In addition unlicensed freebooters could attack. Time and again, owners petitioned governments to grant escort ships or to arrange convoys. They faced

Left: Seal of James Hutchinson, a York merchant trading from Danzig in 1647.

Below: Letter from James Hutchinson, dated 1647 and describing difficult trading conditions: 'noe hopes heare of selling anythin'.

natural hazards, too, such as storms which caused cargoes to shift and ships to founder, and uncharted reefs and sandbanks which even the experienced mariner could not always avoid.

The merchants had to restrain their own members from taking advantages. In 1579, following the 'unfriendly dealing' of the town of Hamburg and the other Hanses restraining the English merchants from their accustomed traffic, a decision had been made to choose the town of Emden as the destination for the shipping of the fellowship. Penalties were set out for infringement and to deter 'dyvers dysordered bretheren respecting more their private lucre and gayne then the contynuance or mayntennance of the general estate in prosperitie and welfare'. An oath had been devised to which all brethren had to subscribe upon penalty of £20. The Act was ordered to be distributed so that no one could plead ignorance.

The correspondence also includes some smaller administrative problems, important for the people concerned. In 1570 there was a letter from the deputy and officers of Merchants Adventurers of England written from Hamburg to the Governor of the same in York asking for an investigation of the case of a hapless apprentice, Thomas Hewitson, whose master had died and whose widow refused to certify his 'faythfull good & Just servyce' despite the fact that four York merchants had vouched for him. These merchants were asked to examine the widow and if she made prejudicial allegations against the young man, to ascertain 'whether all the same be trew or by her onely uttered of evell wyll'.

The archive includes 23 letters from James Hutchinson, writing from

Danzig to Joseph Oley in Konigsberg in the mid-17th century. Both men were Merchant Adventurers of York and members of the Eastland Company. James was the nephew of a Lord Mayor of the same name to whom he had been apprenticed. He was only about 29 years old when he arrived in Danzig. The letters show a conscientious and industrious man trying to forge a living in difficult economic circumstances. He kept track of shipping movements and reported on sales and prices and the state of trade. In April 1647 he wrote: 'I feare som of our Cuntrymen are depe in as £12,000 or £13,000 … bad hopes of any good markits'.

He suspected the activities of two Scots, said to be broke, who left him with scant chance of getting the money owed to him. 'It shall be caveat to me,' he wrote bitterly, 'to trust a Scott noe farther as I can throw him by the heles'. The financial arrangements for trading consisted of the straight exchange of cash, barter for commodities required to be shipped to England (for example rye, hemp, flax, potash) and bills of exchange which were subject to fluctuations in currency if payment was delayed for long.

He also had worries about some of the cloths he was selling, fearing that the quality was not always adequate and not wanting to cheat his buyers. He complained of bayse and kerseys (coarse woollen cloth) 'soe baysely mayde … that I feare I shall not sell them'. On a lighter note, Hutchinson sent to another York merchant residing in Konigsberg two stoups of sack (a Spanish wine), and to Joseph Oley, two stoups of Rhine wine and '6 Lemmons … if suger be to be had'.

The merchants' correspondence may relate a tale of woe and unfair treatment, but their trade was prosperous enough in the long term to sustain them and enrich some. In fact for 1646, cloth imported into the Baltic was valued at approximately £128,000, which was 50 times higher than that for hides and the skins, the next highest export from England, although this was considerably lower than the trade in 1625. The letters show the complexity faced by the York merchants seeking to maintain their trading position in the hard commercial world.

attorney and notaries had been appointed to ensure the fraternity's business ran smoothly. Work proceeded apace on the Hall, under the supervision of the head carpenter, John Craneby, and the chief plasterer, John Bolton. Other workmen – carpenters, plasterers, tilers and labourers – were supplied with beer and paid a daily rate. With cartloads of wood, lime, plaster and tiles arriving regularly, it must have been a busy site. The fraternity spent £90, a considerable sum, on the building in 1357, and although expenditure fell the following year, it rose again to £123 in 1359. Clearly, the funds were already in place and the project seems to have been impressively well organised from the start (*see Chapter 5*).

The result, a hall that has survived for more than 650 years, is a testament to the energy and vision of those who built it. Who were they? The fraternity was open to both men and women, and although many women appear to have joined with their husbands, they and widows were members in their own right. A significant number of mercers and merchants were certainly members from the beginning, but this may reflect the fraternity's connection with St Crux church and the fact that many merchants lived in the area around Pavement. Other members in the early years included a cook, a baker, a butcher, an ironmonger, a bower, a skinner and a tiler. John of Scarborough, a painter, was a member, as was the vicar of Poppleton and the chaplain of Howke. The core membership may have lived in the same neighbourhood, and have known each other in the street or in church. Perhaps they had kin or commercial connections, or simply shared a concern for the inadequate provision of charity locally. Whatever linked them, they formed an association with the imagination and drive to raise a hall that still serves today to promote their original aims of charity, fraternity and religion.

Their achievement is all the greater when we consider that these were not the powerful merchant members of the civic elite who became associated with the Hall in the later 15th and 16th centuries. Master of the fraternity in 1357 and 1358, John Freboys was a shopkeeper who lived in Petergate at the time of his death. He held civic office as a chamberlain and bailiff, but was never mayor as so many of his successors in the next centuries were. Nor were any other of the founders of the fraternity. Given their relative lack of wealth or status within the city it is

A wooden corbel in St Anthony's Hall shows a medieval merchant wearing his distinctive merchant's hat.

all the more remarkable that they envisaged a hall on such a scale, especially if we consider that less than ten years earlier, the Black Death had ravaged the country. The experience of living through the plague must have been a vivid memory still in the minds of all the first members, and may well have driven their preoccupation with the fate of their souls after death.

York, in fact, experienced a period of economic expansion after the Black Death, and attracted immigrants to the city to replace the population that had died. The fraternity, too, prospered, and attracted members from as far away as Newcastle, Whitby and Hull. By 1371 it was able to apply for a licence to expand its work and found a hospital in the Undercroft. The new foundation was confirmed in 1373 by Archbishop Thoresby who detailed its organisation. Initially the hospital was to offer care to 13 'poor and feeble' persons whose spiritual and physical welfare would be in the charge of a chaplain appointed as Master with a salary of ten marks a year, but as funds became available, more chaplains would be appointed and places offered to more inmates. The office of the dead was to be recited every day, while the seven penitential psalms with prayers for the king, patron and benefactors of the hospital were to be said three times a week.

The emphasis on the spiritual underlines the fact that the hospital was primarily a religious institution, albeit under secular supervision. Members of the fraternity remained closely involved in the affairs of the hospital, and presumably continued to use the Great Hall for their own meetings and social activities. Four brethren were elected to administer the hospital, to appoint the Master or Warden, and to pay the salaries of the chaplains and any expenses. Hospital business was authorised with a seal depicting the Coronation of the Virgin, with the legend *sigillum commune hospitaliter* [sic] *fratrum et sororum beate Marie virginis juxta pontem Fosse Ebor* (the common seal of the hospital of the brothers and sisters of the Blessed Virgin Mary next to Foss Bridge, York). The seal and its matrix are still in the possession of the Company.

Although the hospital, like the guild, was founded in honour of Our Lord Jesus Christ and the Blessed Mary, it came to be known as Trinity hospital, a name that was still in use in the 19th century. Little is known of its history in the last quarter of the 14th century, but evidently the hospital continued to grow and by 1396 it was managed by two chaplains and five brethren, and owned four houses, nine cottages and seven shops as well as the Hall and buildings on the same site. Fifteen years later, the warden was assisted by two chaplains and two clerks, while the number of inmates had more than doubled.

The Undercroft, looking towards the Chapel.

A further licence was obtained in 1411, this time for the Chapel that had been rebuilt in place of the original one that had evidently fallen into disrepair and was described as 'ruinous'. The new Chapel served the hospital but was also a focus of devotion for members of the fraternity, who over the years gifted many fine vestments, ornaments and images in another tradition that has continued to the present day. The present Chapel east window, appropriately showing scenes of charity, fraternity and religion, is a modern work in memory of John Saville (Governor 1961–2).

The Mystery of Mercers:
The Mercers' Guild, 1430–1581

The distinction between mercers and merchants is a subtle one. Theoretically, a mercer dealt in 'mercery', small manufactured goods, usually luxury textiles, but he might also work closely with any number of producers. Robert Collinson, a mercer who died in 1458, left to the 'dyers, fullers, shearmen and weavers working with me, from whom I have had any goods, a good breakfast and 12d. each.' A merchant, in 14th-century York at least, was more likely to be trading wholesale in overseas markets. But mercers frequently expanded the scope of their operations and imported cloth and accessories in their own right, in which case they might be referred to as a merchant, while if business contracted, there was little difference between them and chapmen. When Henry VI granted them a charter to form a mystery, or guild as it is more commonly known today, in 1430, members included a range of tradesmen – chapmen, drapers, spicers, vintners, mercers and merchants – all of whom acted to some extent as middlemen between producers and consumers. Unlike the craftsmen who manufactured goods on their premises, members of the mercers' mystery were primarily dealers, some specialised, like the spicers and vintners, and others trading in whatever came their way.

The distinctions between them were blurred, but nonetheless real. Merchants were generally wealthier and of higher status. Commonly they traded overseas. Wool, which dominated exports from York in the 14th century, was gradually replaced by cloth in the 15th century as the cloth-making industry expanded, but merchants rarely specialised and were always on the lookout for a good deal. Enterprise, according to Sylvia

Thrupp in her study of medieval London merchants, was what distinguished merchants from their contemporaries: 'Wherever there was gain to be had, there were merchants to bid for it or intrigue for it.' The success of the merchants of York can be measured by their growing political importance. At the beginning of the 14th century, merchants appear to have played little part in civic government, but in the second half of the century at least 19 of the 26 mayors of York were merchants and engaged in some form of foreign trade.

Not all of these men, however, were associated with the Hall. The wealthiest of York merchants did not begin to join the Mercers' Guild until after 1440. As members of the fraternity, mercers and merchants of more modest means had been closely involved with the Hall from the outset. Their incorporation as a formal guild may have been seen as a way of formalising an association that already existed, and perhaps of furthering their own political and economic interests without interference from a city Corporation that consisted largely of their more successful fellows.

Certainly, they invested a good deal of money and time to obtain the charter. John Lillyng made three trips to London, where a considerable amount of greasing of palms seems to have gone on. Lillyng, a mercer of questionable reputation (*see box, p.21*), spent 40s. on 'wyne and dyners' for lawyers and clerks. Other officials received cash payments, including £3. 6s. 8d. to the Lord Chamberlain, and 6s. 8d. to Stanley, 'his man'. The charter itself and the seal cost the mercers £5. There were other expenses too, for green wax, wine and cakes, and no fewer than two lost horses. Lillyng appears to have been a persuasive character, and he and John Burnlay, who accompanied him, were rewarded later with grants 'for thaire gode labour and busyness that they did for the company'.

The result of their efforts was a charter granted by Henry VI in 1430 'to the men of the mystery of mercery of the city of York' ('*pro hominibus mistere mercerie civitatis Ebor*') incorporating them as a guild. This made them independent of the Corporation and enabled them to regulate their own affairs and

A panel of stained glass dating from the early 20th century in the Governor's Parlour showing Ouse Bridge and King's Staith as they may have looked in the medieval period.

JOHN LILLYNG, A MAN OF EXCELLENT CONNECTIONS AND NEFARIOUS ACTIVITIES

Entrusted with the important task of securing a charter from Henry VI for the Mystery of Mercers (*see opposite*), John Lillyng was obviously a capable emissary. The records show that he was a hospital brother in 1420, but he was also a member of the civic elite, elected Chamberlain (one of the city treasurers) in 1418, and one of the two city Sheriffs in 1420–1. A man of his name entered the prestigious Corpus Christi Guild in 1438–9. However, he was involved in a remarkable case recorded in extensive detail in the city's records.

'Foule deceyte'

In 1427, a rumour arose in York that false osmunds (pointed pieces of iron originally from Sweden) were being manufactured within the city and Lillyng was accused. A search of his house revealed two barrels of new made osmunds of dross mixed in with good ones. He responded that iron was 'skant and dere' but that he had much dross and landiron and he forged the materials into the shape of osmunds for trading it into Iceland and Hull and other places. Lillyng had also sold false tin (being mixed tin, lead and pewter) to the girdlers. He said in his defence that he had bought the tin off a man in London whose name he did not know. He was also accused of blending plaster or lime with his alum and deceiving the litsters (dyers). One York litster stated that if he had used it, the lime would have burnt out the lead bottom of his container. Lillyng was impeached before the Council which included four hospital brothers like himself and the Mayor of the Staple and Calais. They declared that he had caused 'ryght grete harme of ye kynges people and ryght gret sklaundre of ye cite of York'.

He was ordered to find surety of 500 marks (one mark being 13s. 4d.) and also that he should bear the King's Peace to the two witnesses against whom he had threatened bodily harm, on pain of another 500 marks. He was also disenfranchised so that he could neither buy nor sell.

But the seemingly straightforward tale unfolds as he brings in his powerful advocates: no less than the Archbishop of York and the Queen (Katherine of Valois, widow of Henry V and mother of the young King Henry VI). Both sent their emissaries to plead for Lillyng to be spared and the Queen's letter is copied into the book. The Council was not able to resist this show of influence and his frauds were declared void and the financial penalties dropped on condition that he would from henceforth 'be of gude governaunce and trew in all hys bying and hys sellyng wyth outen any gylory, fraude or deceyt … to doo and by and sell after treu cource of merchantdyse.' He had apparently got off scot-free. Nothing further is heard of his activities, but perhaps the Council did not dare try to prosecute him again and bring the might of the Church and State upon their heads.

What was the nature of the relationship between Lillyng, the Archbishop and the Queen? Dr Maud Sellers mentions the sending of lead from Hull to London for the repair of royal and other great houses. This extraordinary story is told in over six closely written pages in the city's Memorandum Book. The Council felt a need to record its actions drawing back the curtain on fraud and of subsequent manipulation of the processes of justice nearly 600 years ago.

Below: One of the six pages relating to the trial of John Lillyng. From the York Memorandum Book A/Y folio 265r. Reproduced from an original held by City of York Council Archives and Local History.

Below right: Accusation of 'foule deceyte' against John Lillyng for trading in substandard iron, tin and alum.

transact their own business under a common seal, which was acquired in 1435 at a cost of 3s.

The Mercers' Guild retained a close association with the hospital in the Hall they shared. When the ordinances of the mystery were written down in 1495, the oath of initiation notes that new members had to swear to be a 'lele [loyal] and trewe brother into the hospitale of the holy Trinite of our Lady Seint Mary and xii apostelles in Fossegate … and favorable and frendeley to all brether and sisters langing [belonging] thereto'. Although there was a clear financial and administrative distinction between the hospital and the mystery of mercers, there was also a considerable overlap in the membership. Richard Kyrkham paid 15s. in 1437 'to be of the company and a brodyr, and Annes his wyf a syster'; this made him a member of the Mercers' Guild, while he and his wife were members of the hospital fraternity. The two associations were so closely interwoven that it is hard to distinguish their activities on many occasions. As in the fraternity, members took an oath of initiation and paid an entrance fee, as well as an annual fee paid quarterly. Women as well as men were accepted into the guild. We know little about how closely they were involved in affairs of the guild, but Marion Kent was a member of the committee formed to consider whether merchants should be allowed to go outside the guild to find vessels to transport their cloth.

Many of the guild's activities were inherited from the fraternity. Like their predecessors, members of the guild were sworn to attend on their three most important religious feast days, of the Trinity (a moveable feast falling on the eighth Sunday after Easter), of the Assumption of the Virgin on 15 August, and of the Annunciation of the Virgin on 25 March. The Chapel was dedicated to the Holy Trinity, and increasingly the Hall was known as Trinity Hall. There was a special service in the chapel on Trinity Sunday, when the Chapel floor was strewn with fresh 'risshis, birk and gales'.

The service was followed by a feast in the Great Hall. As today, these must have been splendid occasions, the Great Hall blazing with candles, and filled with members colourfully dressed in the guild's livery of gowns and hoods. Peter Brears has written elsewhere about the elaborate dishes that were served at the annual Venison Feast (*see box, p.128*). The feast in 1472 saw tables laden with venison, including a fawn, and

Sir Richard Yorke was Master of the Mercers' Guild in 1475. Detail from his window now in York Minster.

with capons, chickens, pork and other meats. 'Kyddes et bakyng' were also served, along with the jellies and custards that were probably made with the calves' feet, marrow and milk purchased at a cost of 2s. 9d., all washed down with ale and a hogshead of wine. In the accounts of a feast held *c.*1550 there is a reference to 10s. given to 'the players' who were perhaps the predecessors of the City Waits who play at feasts in the Hall today, and if so the sound of music above the hubbub must have added to the festive atmosphere. The tables were covered in cloths and elaborate eating vessels, the walls richly coloured. Remains of painted decoration can still be seen in the Hall, and where not painted the walls were probably hung with tapestries. Seating is likely to have been carefully ordered to reflect status within the guild, with the elite sitting at a long table on the dais, but it would be interesting to know whether other members sat with their wives and apprentices or whether the tables were organised according to gender or status. Either way, the feasts must have been important occasions that through ritual and a vivid sensory experience both reinforced

social hierarchies within the guild and engendered a sense of communal identity.

The medieval year was punctuated by feasts and other rituals, not all of them confined to the Hall. The Mercers' Guild was intimately engaged with the annual pageant of Corpus Christi plays (*see box, p.24*). The plays, each enacting a scene from the Bible and put on by one of the many different crafts or occupations in the city, were performed on pageant wagons that were pulled through the streets of York. As the wealthiest occupation, the Mercers were responsible for the last and most important play, the Doom play. The vivid scenes of the Last Judgement called for spectacle, for elaborate costumes and expensive staging, and these the Mercers' Guild provided. A list of play properties drawn up in 1526 includes a devil's head, a cloud, various angels, an iron set with ropes and wheels, and two 'grett angells', one of which was missing a wing. The depiction of the Last Judgement in the Bolton Hours, an early 15th-century manuscript made in York for a wealthy mercantile family, tallies in all its details with the description of the merchants' play and allows us a glimpse of the impact of the pageant that brought the scene to life in the streets of medieval York.

The production of the play was organised by the guilds' Pageant Masters, who were appointed each year to collect the 'pageant silver'. This was a financial contribution from members which was used to buy and repair props and costumes, to hire players and to provide the 'kakkys and ale' at the first rehearsal in 1472 and 'our dynner and drynke to the players' afterwards. The Pageant Masters were key officers in the guild. Listed regularly from 1485, they later became responsible for organising the annual venison feast, which after the Reformation took the place of the mystery plays as the highlight of the guild's

ceremonial year. Both the plays and the venison feasts were revived in the 20th century.

The charitable impulse of members of the Mercers' Guild was just as strong as for members of the earlier fraternity. They gave money to the 'power folks of the horspytall', and heard petitions from those like Humphrey Hogson, who in spite of being treated by two surgeons 'cold get noe remydy' for his broken arm and was left 'wilinge to have [it] seperated from my body, this beinge a dead arme to me, who neither can get my clothes of nor on'. Their generosity was not confined to the poor and the sick. The merchants also appear to have supported education. The foundation of the hospital in 1373 had provided for two poor scholars to receive 4d. a week, and in 1576 John Barker asked for help to keep his son at university in Cambridge, given that the company 'do allowe unto certeyne scollers some annytie towardes helpe in the unyversite'. The support of education is another tradition that continues to this day.

If the members of the Mercers' Guild shared their predecessors' charitable concerns, their devotion was equally fervent, and many generous gifts and bequests were made to the Chapel: glass windows, embroidered vestments, missals and altar cloths. Elizabeth Newton gave two cloths for the high altar showing 'our Lorde syttyng on the rayne bowe, and the coronacon of oure Lady, the grounde of blewe', and there were many other similarly beautiful objects in the Chapel.

While the Mercers' Guild may have echoed the fraternity's aims of charity, fraternity and religious devotion, its primary purpose was as a mystery, that is, an association intended to safeguard the interests of its mercer and merchant members. Its organisation was set out in the ordinances recorded in 1495. The ordinances regulate a wide range of business activities, from trading overseas to setting up shop in York, from 'wrang wrytyng' of contracts to the settling of disputes, and from the swearing of oaths to the terms of apprenticeship.

A master was elected every year to maintain the freedoms and liberties 'of the craft of merchaund and mercery of York'. Together with two elected constables, the Master had to manage the financial affairs of the company and supervise the administration of the hospital. Later Masters assumed outright control of the hospital, calling

The Company and the York Cycle of Mystery Plays

'The said pageants are maintained and supported by the commons and the craftsmen of the same city in honour and reverence of our Lord Jesus Christ and for the glory and benefit of the same city.'

The cycle of plays was always called the Corpus Christi Play in contemporary records. Falling between 21 May and 24 June, depending upon the date of Easter, the 50 or so separate pageants produced by the 'mysteries' or craft guilds were deemed to make up a single play commencing with the Creation and ending with a dramatic performance of the Mercers' play of the Last Judgement. In modern times it is known as the York Cycle of Mystery Plays. The performances took place at regulated stations or stopping places, moving from the gates of Holy Trinity Priory down Micklegate, along Spurriergate, Coney Street, down Stonegate, Petergate, Colliergate and finally ending at Pavement, a route that took the pageant wagons past the most symbolically important places in the city.

The Mercers' pageant was the grand finale with the production of Doomsday or the Last Judgement. Good and evil souls were either judged and taken to heaven with God and his angels, accompanied by heavenly music, or forced into hell where 'to payne endles thei schall be broght'. The mercers did not act in the play themselves and in 1462 their accounts show that 18s. 2d. was paid to the actors and there were other similar payments. Every guild member contributed annual sums called 'pageant silver' towards the maintenance and production of their play. Pageant Masters were chosen or elected annually and were officially responsible for all aspects of getting the play out. The Mercers' records include a bond of 1454 in which Robert Hewyk, who was Parish Clerk of Leeds and a known producer of drama, together with a York tapiter (coverlet maker) and a York weaver are charged with bringing out the pageant called Doomsday upon forfeit of £10.

An indenture of 1433 was found in the offices of Gray's solicitors in York in 1971. It is in the form of a formal agreement between the Master and Constables of the Company of Mercers and the four Pageant Masters of that year for the delivery of the

'gere' belonging to the play and its safe return. It lists all the properties.

In view of the importance of the final play and the wealth of the Mercers, the pageant scenery would have been more elaborate than that of other guilds. There were painted curtains, pieces of timber rainbow, blue and red clouds, gold sunbeams, stars, great and small angels – some painted gold, others red, and even some puppet angels able to run about in heaven by means of a cord. It all conjures up a delightful and colourful picture of medieval drama. Actors wore masks; those of the three devils being double-sided and God's being gilt. He wore a tunic described as 'wounded' and this would have been painted with the wounds of Christ. Instruments are mentioned for the angelic music.

In 1502 Thomas Drawswerd, who came from a family which had for three generations worked in alabaster and marble, was commissioned and admitted to the guild gratis, for renewing the pageant wagon

*Bond for bringing out the performance of
(or producing) the merchants' play, 1453–4.*

*'The Last
Judgement'
performed by
Pocklington School
outside St William's
College in July 2010.*

and all its properties. It must have been impressive and was used in a show in 1541 to greet King Henry VIII on his visit to the city.

The last performance of the cycle was in 1569. Religious sensitivities after the Reformation and visitations of sickness and plague led to their demise. The end of the plays must have been a great disappointment to the populace as the day was an important holiday. A light had gone out in the city and it was to be nearly 400 years before the plays were revived.

Modern performances of the Plays

The first staging of the abbreviated cycle encompassing the whole of the biblical story took place for the Festival of Britain in 1951. Performed in the open air and directed by E. Martin Browne, Director of the British Drama League, the plays were set against the imposing backdrop of St Mary's Abbey. Canon Purvis had produced a modernised version of the text (published in 1951) and this formed the basis of the performances.

The ambitious plan was to work with local amateur theatre groups to produce the cycle of plays every day for two weeks, a truly demanding schedule. The two leading roles of Christ and Satan were performed by professional actors. The tragic unfolding of the drama leading to the Crucifixion against the darkening sky and the medieval walls of the Abbey was something never to be forgotten by those who witnessed it. A great swathe of the people of York was involved with the plays in one role or another and there was a sense of communal effort for the common good and the prestige of the

city, just as one imagines there was in medieval times.

The plays were performed as part of the York Festival every three years until 1969, then mainly every four years. The 1992 and 1996 productions took place in the Theatre Royal and the millennium performance was magnificently staged in York Minster. Thereafter selected wagon plays (which had always run alongside the main productions) represented the ancient drama on a much smaller scale. York schools and the Universities of York and Lancaster played a significant part.

In 1998 there began the association between the Guilds of York and various city drama groups to present an abridged version of the cycle (ten to 12 plays) at four or five stations within the city. The Company of Merchant Adventurers commissioned the York Settlement Players, directed by Richard Digby Day, to mount the Last Judgement in 1998, 2002 and 2006. In 2010 Pocklington School, with which the Company has strong links, took up responsibility for the play.

The modern productions of the plays have now been going for nearly 60 years and it is to be hoped that the ancient words spoken by generations of actors will continue to be proclaimed far into the future. New audiences will experience the Bible stories, portrayed as they were in medieval times and ending with the dramatic climax of the Merchants' play: God divides the souls of humankind between heaven and hell. Angels blow their trumpets on one side whilst, on the other, shouting devils seize and drag away to an eternity of wretchedness those who have been rejected – upon which God reflects:

*Every creature now to call
Lewd and learned, being all here
Receive their doom this day they shall
Every man that ere had life
Be none forgotten great or small …
To every man as he hath served me.*

themselves, as Richard Yorke did in 1475, 'Master of the mistery of merchants and of the gild and fraternity of the Holy Trinity', although this was not without opposition from the chaplains who also considered themselves masters of the hospital. The question as to who held the ultimate authority over the admission of inmates and the running of the hospital seems to have been a source of some friction at times. After 1529, the Master was referred to as the Governor, a title that has remained to the present day.

Master or Governor, the leader of the Mercers' Guild was required to present his accounts every year on 25 March, the feast of the Annunciation of the Virgin, a date that until the 18th century marked the start of the new year. For many years the Company's main court continued to be held on or around 25 March, although it is now held in April to allow a little more time to prepare the annual accounts. The financial records were carefully scrutinised by the membership. When the accounts of Christopher Herbert's three-year governorship were audited in 1575, he was found to have claimed twice for expenses in connection with 'letters concernyng Spayne' and he had to hand over 3s. 4d. to the new Governor, Robert Brooke, in the presence of the auditors.

The guild's money was held in a common box which could only be opened with the knowledge of the Master and both constables. A clerk was employed to draw up the annual accounts, take minutes of meetings and write letters, and thanks to their careful record-keeping, many of these letters, accounts and memoranda still survive and are kept in the archives (see 'Archives' in Chapter 6). This is particularly true of the 15th century, which saw an expansion in

The Last Judgement from The Bolton Book of Hours, fo. 208r.

Panels from the east window in the chapel, installed in 1999 in memory of John Saville (Governor 1961–2), representing his service to youth, charity and the care of the sick.

record-keeping generally, reflected in the acquisition of storage chests and the provision of administrative space. The guild took its business seriously. In 1436 it paid 6s. 8d. for 'a kyste bunden with iren', which is still in the Hall, in the Governor's Parlour, and additional security was later provided with the purchase of 'twa keys to a kyst and to a doyre'. A late 15th-century inventory of furniture in the Hall notes one 'irynbound kist of Pruce makyng' and another iron-bound chest, possibly the one bought in 1436, that was used 'for evydence' in 'the tresour house'.

Detail of the evidence chest, once used to store documents and now in the Governor's Parlour. Dating from the 1340s, the chest was purchased by the Mercers' Guild in the early 15th century and was described in a 1488 inventory as a 'long kyst of waynescott'.

Four times a year, on the medieval Quarter Days, courts were held in the Great Hall and provided an opportunity to discuss business and settle grievances. The new Master was elected, and accounts for the previous year presented, at the feast of the Annunciation of the Virgin in March. The three other Quarter Day courts were held on the Fridays following the Nativity of St John the Baptist on 24 June, known as the Synxon Court, Michaelmas on 29 September and Epiphany on 6 January. All members were expected to attend and were fined if they failed to do so. Fines amounting to 20d. were collected in 1433 from 'diverse persones of the cumpany' who had not appeared before the Master and the rest of the company 'atte x of belle at Trinite halle in the court day'.

An important part of the courts' business was ensuring that trade in the city was properly regulated. Like the craft guilds, the mercers appointed two or four responsible members as searchers with the authority to examine 'all the craft of mercere' in York, whether the traders were members of the guild or not. In an early form of consumer watchdog, they inspected 'all yerdwands, and weghtes and messors' against the standard issued by the government of the day (*see 'Weights and Measures' box, p.49*). Anyone found to be using false weights and measures escaped with a warning on the first occasion, but if they repeated the offence faced a fine of 6s. 8d. which went into the guild's coffers.

The guild, in fact, policed all forms of trading in the city. No one could set up a shop unless they had been admitted to membership of the guild, as William Scott the elder discovered in the 1570s when he 'opnyd shopp in this citie before he was free of this felloship'. On completion of his apprenticeship, a new mercer had to pay 'a resonable payment' agreed by the Master and constables, and be presented to the guild by his own master before he could set up his own shop or warehouse. The regulations were a little more relaxed for the son of a member. As long as he was 'of good governmente', he could set up shop for 3s. 4d.

Hawkers, those who sold their goods outside a shop, were not encouraged. A freeman was only allowed to carry merchandise around the city if he had been sent for by a lord, a knight, 'or any other worthie man', or by a woman lying in childbed. In any other circumstances, he was fined 6s. 8d., and to encourage people to keep an eye open for such offences, half the fine would go to whoever reported him. Strangers, that is anyone who was not a freeman of the city, were even more restricted. They were forbidden to go to

any houses and could only hawk their wares in the common market on market days, on pain of a 40s. fine to the guild.

No member of the guild was allowed to open shop on Sundays or feast days through the year, except on the feast of St Thomas the Apostle. Shopkeepers could also open every day between the feast of the Purification of Our Lady and Easter to sell 'vitayle and lentynstore' if they so desired, but otherwise any flouting of the Sunday opening rule incurred a fine that increased after the first offence.

Policing all these regulations was a challenge. The guild was jealous of its rights and privileges, and in seeking to enforce the ordinances at every opportunity, it had to rely largely on informers. It was concerned to keep all its business confidential, and breaches of that confidentiality were treated very seriously. Anyone 'resonably proved' to have passed on the business of any master or servant of the guild to the customer, whether in York or overseas or anywhere else would be fined 40s., and as an added incentive to stamp out

Below left: These scales dating from the 18th century were used to check weights against the national standard. Similar checks were carried out by searchers from the Mercers' Guild in earlier periods.

Below: 15th-century merchants, from a manuscript in the Bibliothèque Nationale, Paris.

PROPERTIES IN FOSSGATE

The row of shops and flats at nos. 36 to 43 Fossgate are all that remain of the Company's properties in 21 streets and parishes in York, and in Alne, Burnby, Hull, Scagglethorpe and Skelton. They are now Grade 2 listed buildings, the earliest dating from about 1812, although no. 42 contains a crown-post roof truss, probably from the 15th century. It has long been believed that the legal costs resulting from the Company's failure to win the Harwood case (*see p.60*) led to the sale of the bulk of its properties, but in fact most of them had already been lost by this date and the bill for the defence was met by the sale of a single property on Hull Road.

Left: *Entrance to the Merchants' Hall, York, by Edwin Ridsdale Tate (1862–1922).*

Below: *Fossgate in the early morning, showing the surviving Company properties, all painted green.*

Opposite: *The medieval walls of the Undercroft still have niches which may have been used by the hospital inmates to place candles or store their possessions.*

any such indiscretions, 20s. of the fine would go to whoever reported the offence 'for his labor'.

The need to protect confidentiality was part of a general concern with the guild's reputation and public image in the eyes of the wider community. The guild sought to control members' public behaviour as well as their business practices. Slandering another member was particularly frowned upon. Members in conflict with each other had to seek the arbitration of the guild before resorting to law. The 1495 ordinances stipulated a 6s. 8d. fine for any member 'fer any old wreth or newe hanging betwen hym and another of the company, callyng him fals, or lye hym, or fall at debate with hym in the mercery or in eny other place of the cite', and there was swift punishment for violent words or behaviour in the Hall itself.

Such regulations were part of a broader movement towards greater social control. Outside the Hall, all the guild members belonged to a number of other overlapping communities, of street, parish and ward, all underpinned by the same expectations of behaviour. Many of them were also civic officers. Throughout the existence of the Mercers' Guild, and particularly from the mid-15th century onwards, the authorities were preoccupied by the threat of disorder, and these concerns were echoed in the guild of which so many of them were members. The mercers' ordinances promoted the social ideals of measure, order and courtesy appropriate to their status. Merchants were expected to be dignified, to show restraint and respect for authority, and to greet each other according to a code of manners that acknowledged the hierarchy of relationship between the individuals concerned, thus distinguishing themselves from the lower orders of society. The medieval *Ancrene Rewle* described the 'poon [poor] pedlar, who carries nothing but soap and needles, shouteth and calleth out clamorously what he beareth; and a rich mercer goes along quite silently'.

Rituals of oath-taking, feasts, divine services and the formal courts were all designed to reinforce a sense of communal identity, but the guild operated, too, on a practical level. Properties had to be repaired to ensure an income for the hospital; the Hall had to be maintained. The accounts for this period make for interesting reading, showing as they do the various improvements that were made to the Hall over the years (*see Chapter 5*) as well as the day-to-day business

of collecting rents and fines, paying clerks, arranging meetings and enforcing regulations. It is likely that individual members also used the Hall for meetings, to bargain and negotiate and make deals, to call in favours and propose alliances, to impress and perhaps on occasion to intimidate. Oaths and agreements must surely have taken on an extra resonance in the imposing surroundings of the Great Hall. This would have been as true for a merchant in 1420 as it was for his descendant in 1581. The archives show that in spite of the economic depression into which York plunged in the 15th century, and which lasted well into the 16th, many aspects of guild life remained relatively unchanged. There were still feasts, still fines, still wheeling and dealing. Goods continued to be imported and exported. Money was made. The everyday administration of the guild and the Hall ticked along as it had done from the beginning.

And yet this period was split by one of the greatest upheavals English society has ever seen. Today, the Reformation is regarded as marking the break between the medieval and the modern. Perhaps wisely, given the authoritarian nature of the Tudor regime, contemporaries kept their opinions about events to themselves in official records, and the exact consequences of Henry VIII's break with Rome are still a matter of debate among historians. For the Mercers' Guild itself, the Chantries Act of 1547 must have had a profound effect. As religious institutions founded on the belief in intercessory prayers, the hospital and the Chapel that had inspired devotion from its members for so long came under direct threat. Craft associations, however, were generally exempted from the Act, and the merchants duly emphasised the guild and charitable function of the Hall and glossed over the fact that the property assets properly belonged to the hospital. When the hospital was surveyed, the merchants acknowledged that its founder, John Rowclyff, had endowed it with one house but claimed, somewhat speciously, that 'none other person sithens that time hath purchased any more landes' and that the charter of 1430 had given the 'governour and kepers of the mysterye of merchaunts' the right to the hospital property. Their pragmatism was largely rewarded. The merchants held onto the Hall and its properties, and the hospital continued to function, but their arguments were not entirely accepted. In 1587 they still had to prove their ownership of the Hall to agents of Elizabeth I, and they continued to pay rent to the Crown for the chapel until 1830.

The riches were stripped from the Chapel, and the heart went out of the pageant plays which limped on until 1569, but the inmates remained in the hospital and the social and commercial side of guild life seems to have carried on much as usual. Although it continued to accept women, clergymen, clerks and some other occupations, the guild was increasingly dominated by merchants whose business interests lay primarily overseas in the Baltic states (*see box, p.32*). The relationship between the York merchants and the Baltic was played out against a backdrop of economic depression in the 15th century. Henry VII, not a king noted for his sentimental approach to such matters, remitted half the city's fee-farm in 1486, having seen for himself 'the great ruyne and extreme decay' into which the city had fallen. There was still a widespread perception of poverty well into the 16th century, and as late as 1548 the merchants were declaring that 'the cytye of York is but a pore cytye'.

Nonetheless, there were always merchants who prospered. Men like Christopher Herbert, governor for three years between 1573 and 1575, wielded power and influence in York, but their fortunes were based on trade with the Low Countries. Herbert himself spent some time in Antwerp in the 1560s, negotiating on behalf of the York merchants. All English merchants trading in the Low Countries had to be members of the Merchant Adventurers of England, and to abide by their regulations. There were clear benefits in doing so, but it must have been galling to men of Herbert's ilk to find themselves subservient to the powerful London merchants who dominated the Merchant Adventurers of England. Relations were often strained between the Londoners and the merchants of the northern cities, who struggled to deal with interlopers in their markets, and in the late 1570s the York merchants set about applying for a new charter that would confirm their monopolies.

As with the charter of 1430, this took some time, a number of trips to London, following the court as it moved between Westminster and Richmond, and a good deal of expense. Once again, various middlemen had to be paid: a lawyer, the Queen's attorney, a

servant to the Master of Requests, Mr Garth 'for the charter drawyng' and 30s. to Mr Torney 'for ingrossyng the charter'. The charter was finally granted by Elizabeth I in 1581 and the Mystery of Mercers which had seen such changes in the course of its history was formally incorporated as the Company of Merchant Adventurers of the City of York, a name it has retained to this day.

In the medieval period small ships on the River Foss were able to tie up next to the Hall.

OVERSEAS TRADE

For much of the middle ages, wool was the major English export. The wool trade was so important that it was carefully controlled through the establishment of a wool staple at Calais. A staple was a fixed outlet, and merchants wanting to buy or sell wool in Calais had to be members of the Staple there. A number of wealthy wool merchants from York were Staplers, and some, like Sir Richard Yorke, Master of the Mercers' Guild in 1475, rose to the influential position of Mayor of the Staple of Calais.

Not all merchants wanted to deal in wool, or be restricted to a fixed market. They were then free to risk, or 'adventure', their capital elsewhere, and merchants who traded in these less secure markets were known as 'merchant adventurers'. Although

the business of the merchant adventurer was in reality less swashbuckling than the name suggests, there were nonetheless considerable risks involved in trading outside a staple. Piracy, shipwrecks, disputes with foreign merchants and officials, and wars which led to the disruption of shipping or the closure of markets could make the merchant adventurer's trade a hazardous one.

But there were rewards, too. York merchants shipped goods to places as far away as Iceland and Spain, and imported wine from Bordeaux, but as cloth manufactured in Yorkshire replaced wool as the main export during the 15th century, the most usual destination was the Low Countries. There were four great cloth markets held in Antwerp every year to

'Old Ouse Bridge, York 1784' by Joseph Farington. Before the advent of the railways, most goods were transported by river, and were loaded and unloaded at King's Staith.

mark the four seasons: the Cold market in winter, the Pase in spring, the Synxon market in summer and the Balms in autumn. Each market lasted up to six weeks and drew merchants from all over Europe to buy and to sell. So important were the Low Countries for York merchants that they often left apprentices and factors in cities like Bruges and Middelburg as well as Antwerp to deal on their behalf all year round, while they went over only to supervise sales at the seasonal fairs. The 1495 ordinances of the guild provide for one or two 'honest' members to represent the Master and constables overseas and to have full authority over any of the members' servants or attorneys who were 'mysgovrned', just as if they had been in York.

In those days there were no consulates to represent British interests abroad, and merchants had for a long time banded together in companies or associations known as 'hanses' for mutual protection and support. The Company of Merchant Adventurers of England was dominated by the wealthy London merchants, but its Governor was based in Antwerp, from where the Company could supervise the activities of all the English trading there and negotiate on their behalf, and where they were known as the 'English nation'. All English merchants, including those from York, had to be members of the Company of England if they wanted access to the lucrative markets in the Low Countries. To join, they had to be able to pay the admission fee and submit to regulation of both their trade and

their behaviour by the Company's officers. On the whole, the advantages of membership outweighed the disadvantages, and until 1581, when it was incorporated as a company of merchant adventurers in its own right, the Mercers' Guild acted as a local court of the Company of Merchant Adventurers of England, and maintained a close correspondence with the Governor in Antwerp.

Inevitably there was some friction between the English merchants. Many of the letters in the archives concern the grievances of York and other northern merchants who felt that the powerful Londoners were discriminating against them, but the Company offered a structure to their operations in the Low Countries and much greater influence than they would have had alone, especially when trying to secure trading rights and privileges both at home and overseas. There was rivalry with merchants from other countries who set up similar associations for common profit and advantage. The Easterlings, from the Baltic cities that made up the powerful Hanseatic League, were particularly resented for the privileges they enjoyed. In the 14th and 15th centuries their close relationship with the English crown won them great advantages in handling trade between England and northern Europe. In London, these Hanseatic merchants were based at the Steelyard until they were expelled by Elizabeth I in 1598 in retaliation for the Hapsburg Emperor's prohibition on English merchant adventurers trading in Germany. Their

WILLIAM HART *sometimes pastor of the English Church at Embden, and afterwards at Stode beyond the seas did give 600 pounds to the companie of Merchants Adventurers to be lent to twelve young men exercising the same trade for two yeares, and then to other twelve successivelie for ever. and also 300 to y poore.*

William Hart spent some time in the Baltic as pastor in the English Church. His generous bequest of £600 (the equivalent of more than £46,000 today) as start-up loans for young merchant adventurers was administered by the Company for many years. (Artist unknown, before 1633).

the Baltic, and the Eastland Company provided an opportunity to exploit opportunities to trade with eastern and central Europe as well as Scandinavia. It was an opportunity that the London merchant adventurers were keen to keep to themselves, but the merchants of York and other northern cities persisted in their claims, and they were eventually allowed to join on payment of a fee of £10.

The episode is symptomatic of the tension that often existed between the York merchants and their London fellows within the Company of Merchant Adventurers of England. This was exacerbated after the York merchants were incorporated in their own company. The 1581 charter which gave the York company a monopoly on all imported goods except fish and salt undoubtedly benefited many individual merchants in the city, but they still needed to be members of the English company, or of the Eastland Company if they wished to trade in the Baltic. The overlapping membership requirements can be confusing at times when trying to make sense of the records. By 1616, York had its own branch of the Eastland Company, and in 1628 the national association set up its own residence in York, meeting in the Cloth Hall on Ouse Bridge, taking over all export and import trade in the city. Although many of its members were also members of the Company of Merchant Adventurers of the City of York, from then on the company based at the Hall in Fossgate dealt only with matters of wholesale and retail within York. Its glory days of overseas trading may have been over, but individual members continued to flourish. The 17th century saw a proliferation of trading companies, and it would be interesting to know how the silver cup known as the Bombay Cup came to be in Mumbai Cathedral, and inscribed 'the gift of the Greenland Merchants of the City of York 1632'.

Closer to home, the long trading relationship with Antwerp had come to an end in the 1560s, when war with Spain led to a ban on the import of English cloth into the Low Countries by the Spanish regent there. The English merchant adventurers settled on Emden in East Friesland as their main mart instead, but in spite of the warm welcome they received, they

privileged position until that point provoked envy and resentment among English merchants, who did not receive anything like the same kind of advantages when they were trading in the Baltic. Bitter complaints about the unfairness of the Easterlings' privileges is a constant theme in the merchant adventurers' correspondence (*see box, p.16*).

In spite of the political situation, the 1560s and 1570s were a time of revival for York merchant adventurers. Increased access to the Baltic brought greater prosperity, and trade with Russia was opened up. The Eastland Company was founded in 1579 to challenge the traditional dominance of the Hanseatic League in the Baltic. Membership was initially restricted to English merchants who had traded through the Sound between Denmark and Sweden before 1568. The Sound links the North Sea and

Below left: A party from the Company visited the English Church in Hamburg in 2002.

Below: Stained glass panel in the Governor's Parlour showing ships in a Baltic port.

while younger members of the Company might be corrupted by Popish tendencies in Catholic Antwerp. In Hamburg, they had the opposite problem: 'their preachers inveighe against us and our religion by the name of sacramentaries, sectaries and the like: and herebye doe all that in them lyeth to stirre up and increase the people against us and make us odious unto them.'

Nonetheless, the English appear to have settled comfortably enough in all three cities. They were an established community with their own houses and churches. William Hart, whose portrait still hangs in the Hall, was pastor of the English church in Emden, and the Hamburg Staatsarchiv contains registers of marriages and deaths of York merchants who lived and traded in the city until it was occupied by the Napoleonic forces in 1805. An attempt to re-establish a residence of the Merchant Adventurers of England in Hamburg after the peace of 1815 was unsuccessful, although a colony of English expatriates remained. Their English Church, built in 1836, still survives. The extensive records in Hamburg have yet to be studied in depth; further research would add considerably to our understanding of the links between York and the Baltic, and of the merchants who lived and traded there.

moved back to Antwerp the following year. By 1566, however, negotiations between Philip II and Elizabeth had broken down, and the court of the Merchant Adventurers of England held in Antwerp in March 1567 noted that Hamburg had offered 'dyvers goodly privileges upon hope that we shoulde occupie and use somme trade there, and for the purpose have … prepared a howse for us'. Hamburg became the base of English Baltic trade for the next ten years, after which the English company moved back to Emden. None of the cities was a perfect place in which to settle as far as the English merchants were concerned. They worried that Emden was not powerful enough to protect them against 'the malice of the Hanses',

'FREIGHTED WITH FELLYSSHYPPE': SHIPPING AND THE MERCERS' GUILD

The livelihood of merchants trading overseas was intimately bound up with shipping. The risks of a sea voyage were many: bad weather, fickle winds, piracy, shipwrecks, delays, and interference from the authorities both at home and abroad. English ships were liable to be arrested and used for naval service at times of war, and although the Crown was supposed to pay compensation, in practice payments were often delayed and the ship owner still lost out on more lucrative commercial voyages, not to mention the risk of the ship being damaged or sunk in battle. Ships were at the mercy of overseas officials too, delayed by bureaucracy or confiscated outright, like the *Valentine* of Hull, which was seized by the Danes in 1468 in retaliation for English piracy. But if English merchants wanted access to the lucrative markets on the Continent, they had to go to sea.

The records of the Mercers' Guild are full of references to shipping, many of them hard to interpret in detail. Nevertheless, it is clear that there was a well-established process. Goods were transported between York and Hull on 'keels, bootes and lighteners'. Before they could carry goods, the keel owners had to appear before the Master and constables of the guild and swear that they would keep all members' goods safe and secure down to the last penny. The guild had the authority to exclude or expel any mariners who failed to comply with their regulations and insist that they were 'neuer to saile ony gudes or merchandises of ony person or persons from thensfoirth'.

Rates for river transport were agreed and formalised in an indenture like the one made in 1555 for seven years: a ton of iron, loaded from a ship, cost 2s. 8d., and 3s. if loaded from the shore; a load of red herrings was 2s., of ashes, 20d., and 'a chalder of coles to the marchaunts owne use', 2s. 6d. Transport between York and the coastal ships in Hull was such a vital connection that the York merchants attempted to monopolise river traffic, imposing a two-year boycott on any mariner or shipman who carried goods that belonged to anyone not a member of the guild. The length of the ban had evidently been reduced to a year by the time the mariners petitioned the Mercers' Guild about various problems, ending in an aside 'And also that you wold be so good as to take the Margett of Yorke forth of your boke, for it is a twelmonthe and a daye paste now sence she haithe comitted her offence'.

At Hull, cargo and travellers transferred to a cog or some other kind of sea-going ship. Conditions on board were not as basic as might be expected. Merchants who travelled with their goods took their own food, bedding, chests for storage and servants, while the mariners apparently expected a good diet, with meat on three days a week, and porridge on the others. According to the medieval *Customs of the Sea*, they had bread every evening, with cheese, onions or fish, and wine, prunes or figs.

The ship's cargo was carefully stowed below deck, with all goods secured and the heaviest items at the bottom. Metal blocks and bars would go in first, together with baskets, crates or barrels of worked tin.

Wine, one of the biggest imports to England through the middle ages, was transported in casks called tuns. According to an act of 1423, a tun contained 252 gallons, and it became the standard unit for measuring the carrying capacity of a ship. Thus a quarter of grain took up a quarter of the space a tun would occupy in a ship's hold.

Casks used for carrying liquids as well as 'wet' goods such as herrings, tar or wax, were laid on their sides and fixed with wooden supports to keep them in place. Wool was transported in gigantic sacks weighing 26 stone (164 kg) and sometimes in an even larger load called a 'sarpler', which was the equivalent of two and a half sacks. A 'poke' of wool held half of a normal sack. Grain and salt were also loaded in sacks, while cloth, furs and some spices such as ginger and pepper were carried in bales, a package wrapped in a robust covering such as canvas and secured with cords. Precious fruits were more difficult to transport without damage and were probably packed in rush baskets. The York records also refer to 'packs' of cloth and 'a fatte' of eels.

Measures appear to have varied from place to place. The rates for the transport of goods between Hull and York agreed in 1562 suggest that a quarter in Hull was larger than a quarter in York: 'All manner of grayne Yorke measure the quarter, vjd.; All manner of grayne Hull measure the quarter, vijd.' A chalder of coal to a merchant's house was 'so many coles as ye will spend yearlye', and timber was measured by the 'hundredth'. The most common unit of measurement was the 'last', but this seems to have varied according to the goods it contained.

It was rare for a ship to carry a single commodity, or for a merchant to fill a boat with his cargo, and because of the way goods had to be stowed by type rather than by owner, all packages had to be marked before loading so that they could be identified at the other end of the voyage. To avoid mistaken ownership the Mercers' Guild insisted that

no merchaunt nor mercer beyng a venturer, nor no attorney for them for now forth shall be [buy] no merchaundise on his side see ne beyond, but if the

awner therof sett his own mark therof and no nouther mans mark … that is to say, if it be as a pipe to sett the mark on the pipes hede, and as a barrel on the barrelis hede, and in all oyther merchandise as madder, alame, beere with such like merchaundise to set the mark at both ends.

The Company's ordinances set out in 1603 also insist that members 'sett the right owners mark of the heads or sides of all such waires or marchandize so bought.' A rare example of such a merchant's mark can be seen in two of the stained glass windows in St Martin-cum-Gregory in Micklegate.

The marks were also useful if merchandise was lost overboard in the course of a voyage. When a vessel was in danger of sinking or being stranded, the cargo would be cast overboard (jettisoned) to lighten the ship. Any goods that then floated ashore were known as jetsam. (Flotsam, which is often associated with jetsam, refers to goods that are washed ashore after a shipwreck rather than being deliberately released.) The merchant's mark made it possible to identify whose goods had been thrown overboard and whose had survived. When the *Kattryn* of Hull foundered in 1457, a reckoning was drawn up. The first list notes the amounts for 51 individuals who had 'payd thar jettsone', the second records a further 45 who had 'resseved thar jettsome for the gudes that was kasstyn owtt off the Kattryn off Hull'. Was this a kind of compensation scheme? Some merchants appear on both lists. Lawrence Porter paid £3 7s. 4d. and received 5s. 5d. for a chest and two 'pawtne yryns', while Richard Symson claimed 5s. for a chest and a primer, but paid £6 10s. 11d. for his jetsam.

The 'reknyng' of the *Kattryn* is interesting as it shows how many merchants had an interest in the ship, and the small amount of goods traded by some

Richard Toller's merchant mark, commemorated in stained glass in the nave of St Martin-cum-Gregory.

individuals: one chest, a single harness, two bales of cloth. Given the risks, it was perhaps sensible to spread risks over several ships. The account also demonstrates the variety of merchandise on the ship. As well as the items mentioned above, the *Kattryn* carried wheat, pease, salt, apples, calf skins and 'dyvars parsells'.

The *Kattryn* was an example of a ship chartered on behalf of the Mercers' Guild, which then contracted to furnish it with a full cargo. Although it is not clear exactly how this worked in practice, the many records of payments for 'freighting' in the accounts may refer to collectively organised voyages of this kind. The Guild tried to ensure that the ships were laden as soon as possible. A meeting in the 1470s decided that 'no man of this fellyship doo freyght no shippes … this voyage but these that are freighted with fellysshyppe, that is to say the Laurance, the Hylde, and litill Joorge of Hull … till tyme that the said shippes be resonably laden'.

Not all shipping was organised on a collective basis. Members who arranged their own shipping had to pay a charge known as 'tontight'. This was probably a payment per ton (or perhaps tun) of merchandise, and the amount seems to have varied according to the goods shipped, the size of the ship and the length of the voyage. The guild also collected a payment of 6s. 8d. from ship owners for every overseas voyage, and members were forbidden to load their merchandise until the sum had been paid. Although only a token amount, it was rigorously enforced by the guild. Failure to pay led to a three-year ban on the ship concerned and a £10 fine 'to be imployed to the comon weel of the … Trenete gylde'. It was decided in 1571 that all shipping money should be given towards the relief 'of the power folks of oure hospitall', so fines from shipping may well have been used for the benefit of the poor, reminding us that hard-headed as the merchants of York may have been when it came to commerce, the charitable aspect of their guild was not forgotten.

Extract from the 1457 accounts of the Kattryn *of Hull, recording payments for goods jettisoned in bad weather. Items lost included lead, cloth, calf skins and harnesses.*

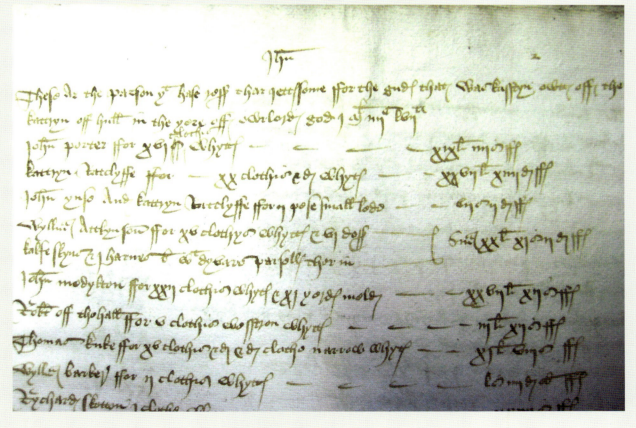

The Company of Merchant Adventurers of the City of York:

1581–1800

CHAPTER 2

The Company of Merchant Adventurers of the City of York

1581–1800

The Charter of 1581 marked a turning point in the Company's history. The York merchants had claimed that a charter would help them recover the prosperity lost as a result of piracy, shipwrecks, the problems caused by the collapse of Ouse Bridge in 1565 after severe flooding, and the competition of merchants who had never been part of the guild but traded 'only to Gratify their Coveteous desire'. The document that Elizabeth I granted, still in the possession of the Company, must have seemed well worth all the effort and expense. Of particular interest to the newly founded Company was the verbose clause which gave them authority not only over its own members but also

> *every other person or Persons intermeddling with the exercise and use or who hereafter shall intermeddle with the Exercise or use of Merchandize or who shall show or expose to sale or permit to be shown or exposed to Sale in his or their house or houses any wares Goods or Merchandize growing, made or imported from beyond the Seas (Fish and Salt only excepted).*

Not unreasonably, the Company interpreted this as giving them a monopoly on trade in all imported goods with the exception of the basic necessities of fish and salt, and it was a privilege they defended vigorously for the next 250 years.

In many other respects, the new Company inherited the organisation of the Mercers'

Guild. A governor and two constables had run the Mercers' Guild since 1430; now the members of the newly chartered Company of Merchant Adventurers of the City of York would elect a governor and a deputy to serve for a year from 26 March, and 'to overlook, Govern and Rule all the Mercers & Merchants of the City … for ever' with the help of 18 elected assistants. There were to be wardens to deal with the Company's property and accounts, and a sergeant, or beadle, to enforce the regulations, just as there had been previously. The Company today is still run by an elected Governor and the Court of Assistants. Like the Mercers' Guild, the new Company was empowered to admit apprentices who had served seven years, or those 'who have followed Merchandize by the Space of ten years and are not

Previous pages: *The Great Hall brilliantly illuminated by the state-of-the-art LED lighting installed in 2009.*

Below: *Seal of Elizabeth I from the 1581 charter. It shows the queen enthroned on one side and on horseback on the reverse.*

Opposite: *The Fossgate entrance to the Merchant Adventurers' Hall has been used for over 650 years.*

Artificers or Handicraftsmen'. It could make and enforce its own ordinances, and appoint searchers to check that correct weights and measures were being used anywhere within the city or suburbs. The crucial difference lay in the monopoly that enabled them to dominate trade in York by insisting that anyone wishing to trade in foreign goods join the Company and pay the appropriate admission fee.

The monopoly undoubtedly benefited individual merchants, but the consequences for the Company as a whole were not so obvious. In order to trade overseas, merchants still had to be members of the Company of Merchant Adventurers of England, or, if they wanted to trade in the Baltic, of the Eastland Company which was founded in 1579 to foster trade with Scandinavia and Baltic Sea states. Until 1581, the Mercers' Guild operated as a local office of these national associations, but once incorporated as a Company in its own right, its concerns narrowed to local trade while the Merchant Adventurers of England and the Eastland Company between them took over all matters relating to international imports and exports (*see box, p.33*). Both companies established separate residences, or local branches, in York, and there may have been a number of other trading companies operating out of the city as well, like the company of Greenland Merchants of the City of York whose gift of a silver cup in 1632 is now in Mumbai Cathedral.

The membership of these different companies frequently overlapped, of course. Unless his business interests were purely local, a York merchant adventurer would also have attended meetings of the national association in the Cloth Hall on Ouse Bridge, and, if he traded in the Baltic, of the Eastland Company. Indeed, the records of both companies are still kept in the Hall, indicating the closeness of the relationship between the three associations throughout the 17th century until a dispute over the governorship of the York Eastland Company caused the closure of the residence in 1696. The necessary association with the Merchant Adventurers of England for York merchants trading overseas may explain why the York company did not apply for its own coat of arms until 1969 but was content to use the arms of the national company to which they also belonged. The distinctions between the three associations may seem obscure to us today,

but to contemporaries they were clearly significant. In 1742, a dispute over precedence arose between two newly elected sheriffs of the city, the grocer Amor Oxley and the bookseller John Hildyard. Oxley claimed precedence 'being a Merchant Adventurer of the City of York', while Hildyard asserted his right 'being free of the Hamburgh Company'. The matter was referred to the Lord Mayor, who decided in favour of Oxley.

As members of the English company, York merchants were still very much involved in trading overseas. Their apprentices and factors were often based abroad, initially in Antwerp, until the Dutch War of Independence with Spain caused the blockade of that market, and then in what is now Germany and the Netherlands, where the English established settled trading communities in cities like Hamburg, Emden or Stade. There was regular travel between York and the Continent. The minutes of a Court meeting held in April 1679 note in the margin that it was held 'when the secretary was at Hamburgh'.

Merchants still tended to be the wealthiest citizens, and they continued to dominate civic politics until the end of the 17th century. While the monopoly undoubtedly gave all members of the Company a commercial advantage over non-members, even for merchants the 17th century was not a period

Left: *The Bombay Cup, made of silver and inscribed 'the gift of the Greenland Merchants of the City of York 1632', is now in Mumbai Cathedral.*

Opposite: *Queen Henrietta Maria visited York in 1643. This 18th-century copy of her portrait by Van Dyck (1599–1641) hangs in the Great Hall.*

Below: *'Prospect of a Noble Terras Walk', – The New Walk, 1756, by Charles Grignion after Nathan Drake. York was a centre of sociability in the 18th century.*

of uninterrupted prosperity, disrupted as it was by plague – with the most severe outbreaks in 1604 and 1631 – and civil war. For a brief time York resumed its traditional role as the military headquarters in English campaigns against Scots, and Charles I even moved his court to the city in March 1642 for six months. The Hall was used to confine Parliamentarian prisoners, evidently in such squalid conditions that Queen Henrietta Maria was moved to give money for their relief on her visit in 1643, a gesture that is commemorated by her portrait which today hangs in the Great Hall. The siege of York in 1644 ended in the surrender of the Royalists, and for the rest of the wars the city remained under Parliamentarian control. Like the rest of the country, York merchants were divided in their loyalties, sometimes bitterly so, but the Company survived the wars with its traditions and its Hall intact. Sadly, the minutes for much of that period are lost, but records of meetings held from 1677 onwards show that the Company continued to function and to fulfil the terms of the 1581 charter.

Perhaps the most noticeable change in the city as far as the Company's members were concerned was the decline of trade during the 17th century. Hull to the east and the cloth towns of the West Riding to the west grew at the expense of York, and as the Ouse became less and less navigable for large boats, the once-busy staiths fell silent and the city dwindled into a minor inland port. And yet, visiting York in 1680, Henry Keepe could write that the inhabitants were 'verry civill and courteous, obliging to strangers who come out of curiosity as well as to forraigners for ther trafick and commerce … I take it to be one of the cheapest citys in Europe'. It remained the social capital of the North and a centre of consumption, and food, clothing and building and furnishing trades flourished as more and more gentry were attracted to the city. The Company's membership diversified in keeping with the times and with the new emphasis on local trade. No longer did merchants and mercers dominate the Company. Grocers, apothecaries and ironmongers were all important enough groups to have their own searchers from 1677 onwards (*see box, p.49*).

The industrialisation that transformed cities like Leeds and Manchester in the 18th century largely bypassed York. Long-established associations like the Company clung to their rights, and those wanting to

Left: *Left: The Deputy Governor and the Clerk collect the ceremonial robes and the Governor's ring after Charter Day Court in April 2010.*

Below: *Although not a member of the Company, Sir Robert Watter's elaborate tomb in St Crux Hall is typical of those commissioned by wealthy merchants of the late 16th and early 17th centuries.*

set up one of the new manufactories went where there were fewer restrictions and booming populations. If the industrial revolution made little impact, the city was nonetheless transformed in the 18th century with new buildings and by a new sense of civility. Other towns might outstrip it 'in trade and hurry of business,' acknowledged the historian Francis Drake in *Eboracum*, his magisterial history of the city published in 1736, 'yet there is no place, out of London, so polite and elegant to live in as the city of York'.

In spite of major social changes in the two centuries that followed the 1581 charter, the concerns of the Company remained remarkably consistent, following the ordinances drawn up in 1603 for 'the good government of the socyitie of marchantes and marcers'. The ordinances tried to regulate members' behaviour just as the Mercers' Guild had done in 1495. No Company business was to be passed on, disputes between members were to be dealt with by the Governor in the first instance, and they were to address each other 'in suche quiet and decent manner as shalbe to be well thought of'. Nor were they to interrupt each other. Anyone standing up in a court 'shall without interruption be suffered to make an end

of his speaches and none to stand up in the meane time, and whosoever doth interrupte anie other (except Mr governor) to pay for everie suche offence xijd [12d.]'.

As in earlier times, members were expected to attend courts and to dress in their Company robes.

WILLIAM ROBINSON

William Robinson was Governor of the Company towards the end of Queen Elizabeth's reign, and his portrait is thus one of the earliest in the collection. His picture is typical of provincial portraiture of this period, the pose somewhat rigid and rather two-dimensional. It is painted on a joined quartered oak panel, which has split vertically through the figure and been restored a number of times. He is shown half-length, the figure set within a painted arch. He wears Governor's or Alderman's robes, a ruff and a black skullcap. On the forefinger of his right hand is a gold ring, which possibly bore his coat of arms. After cleaning, the ghost of a staff appeared in his right hand. Another loss has been the date, since after the letters 'AD' the figure is illegible. However, two other variants of the picture are in other collections (one still with the family) and the date of 1622 is visible, so all three may be posthumous portraits. Robinson's face would not suggest charity, but the inscription tells us that he 'did give 40 pounds to the Companie of Merchants adventurers to be lent to fower young men of the Companie for five yeares and then to others accordinglie for Ever.' The words on these early pictures are spelled as they sounded to the artist, and the pronunciation of 'four' as 'fower' can still be heard in these parts. Robinson's trading ventures brought him a fortune, which he wisely spent on land, buying the great estate at Topcliffe now known as Baldersby Park, and building a Jacobean mansion. He died in 1616, having established a dynasty which would see future direct descendants in nationally important positions. In the 18th century two of the Robinsons (then with the title of Lord Grantham) became ambassadors, and at the beginning of the next century Frederick Robinson was, for a brief time, Prime Minister. His elder brother inherited the title Earl de Grey, and Frederick's son became Marquess of Ripon.

WILLIAM ROBINSON merchant late of the Cittie of York Alderman deceased did give 40 pounds to the companie of Merchants adventurers to be lent to fower young men of the companie for five yeares and then to others accordinglie for Ever. once

Appropriate dress was carefully specified in the 1603 ordinances. All married men, and those who had been chamberlains of the city, were to wear their chamberlain's gowns to all courts, while the Governor and any aldermen were to wear 'ther gownes and tippets' and the rest 'ther ancient citizens gownes'. The wearing of appropriate dress was an extremely important part of life in the pre-modern city, and reflected status on an everyday level as well as on ceremonial occasions. The Council records carefully specified who was to wear what when on civic business. The length and colour of gowns was important, and tippets (strips of cloth attached to the hood of a gown, or perhaps short cloaks of wool or fur that covered the shoulders) were particularly significant status markers.

Certainly, the Company insisted on the correct dress when attending courts, and the minutes are full of fines for those 'comyng to the courte withowte gowens'. It was decided in 1657 that anyone who had not been a chamberlain of the city would not be fined if he came to quarter courts without a gown, while only the Governor, Deputy and the secretary needed to wear gowns to the Court of Assistants. Nonetheless, fines 'for short gownes' are still common in the late 17th century. These fines were known as brogues, and were also imposed for 'absences and late comings to courtes and sermons'. It seems that for certain offences, or perhaps certain individuals, the level of the fine was decided by a vote. When Emmanuel Justice petitioned the court for freedom by redemption in 1691, evidently having been caught selling imported goods, he asked them to take into consideration the fact that he was already a member of the Eastland Company. Three sums were put forward as possible fines: £10, £15 and £20. A show of hands set his fine at £15. Justice was sworn in at the next court for the usual fee of 13s. 4d. Funds raised from brogues such as these were usually given to the poor of the hospital, although a portion was sometimes divided amongst the officers of the Company.

The regulation of local shops would have been familiar to members of the Mercers' Guild, too. The Company was firm in upholding its right to a monopoly on the sale of imported goods, and regularly pursued any traders who refused to pay the cost of admission. A meeting was held in August 1677 to discuss 'severall stuffs and mercery wares haveing bin sold & exposed to sale in the Minster yard by Mr Philips & others not free of the Citie nor company,' and the sergeant was ordered to seize the goods. No exceptions were made. When Mrs Buxton, as executrix, was left to dispose of the goods in John Best's shop, she was hauled up before the Company's court in 1680 for keeping the shop open while not a member herself. She was grudgingly allowed six months in order to dispose of the goods, provided that she bought nothing new to sell. The defence of their monopoly proved a burden for some members, too, and several mercers complained in 1699 about the 'extraordinary charge & expences to suppresse irregular Traders in theire way'.

The Company's case against these 'irregular' shopkeepers rested on the 1581 charter, and there was consternation in 1729 when the charter itself was mislaid. An immediate search was instituted, and the charter was fortunately found before the wardens had to 'have recourse to the Tower of London for a copy'. Once back in their hands, the charter continued to be held over the heads of small shopkeepers who refused to join the Company. Not all were impressed by it.

Mary Tuke opened a tea and grocery shop in Walmgate in 1725 and resisted the Company's attempts to force her to become a member for eight years. Mrs Tuke's shop passed to her great-nephew, who moved into manufacturing cocoa, and it was eventually sold to its manager, Henry Rowntree. Rowntree & Company was a famous company in York for many years and although now part of Nestlé UK Ltd, its chocolates are still made here. Several members of the Rowntree family played an active part in the Company during the 19th and 20th centuries.

Some 50 years after Mrs Tuke's defiance, the aptly named Mrs Doughty was equally resistant to the Company's demand that she should join and pay 10s. a year for the privilege of selling mercery wares in her shop. The Secretary wrote to her in October 1777 to say that the Company was 'determined to proceed against you in a legal manner for exercising the Trade of a Mercer in this City without being free of the said Company'. Mrs Doughty was invited to join the Company and turn up at the next committee

Letter to Mrs Doughty threatening legal proceedings if she continued to trade.

THE COMPANY'S YARDSTICK, WEIGHTS AND SCALES

Maintenance of trading standards has always been one of the main concerns and responsibilities of the Company. The 15th-century Ordinances stipulate that searchers should search throughout the craft of mercers within the city, inspecting all 'yerdwands' and weights. Anyone found in default was warned to amend. If they had not corrected at the second time, they were to pay 6s. 8d. The maintenance of standards was achieved by reference to standard weights and measures held by the Company and a number of these survive in the Merchant Adventurers' Hall collections.

The Company's brass yardstick bears the date 1658 and presumably conforms to the standard established by the Exchequer under Queen Elizabeth I in 1588. It is divided in binary fashion from one side of the mid-18 inch point at 9, 4½ and 2¼ inches, a method widely used in the cloth industry.

Standard weights were issued by the government to towns and cities throughout England in 1588, each marked *1588, 30 Eliz.* The Company has four of what should have been a set of seven bell weights, 28lbs, 14lbs, 7lbs and 4lbs, each with small roses stamped on them which may have been county markings. There should also have been a set of disc weights but these,

too, have not survived, though the type is represented in the Merchant Adventurers' collections by 16 disc weights given to it in 1996.

The Company's scales, often displayed in front of the Court tribunal, were bought in 1790 from Charles de Grave, 'seale-maker to his Majesty' in Aldersgate, London, and were evidently serviced by the same firm over 120 years later at the request of the then archivist Dr Maud Sellers.

Above: *Detail from brass yardstick.*

Above right: *Set of proof bell weights. Lead was added to the base as necessary to ensure accuracy.*

Right: *Detail from the Company's scales. See p.28 for full view.*

meeting, and the letter ends on a sinister note: 'If you pay no regard to this Letter blame yourself for the consequences.' The letter, however, did not have the intimidating effect it clearly intended. Mrs Doughty informed the Secretary in no uncertain terms that she was free of the Taylors' Company 'and that was what she should stand by, as her (late) husband told her to stick by that.'

The likes of Mrs Tuke and Mrs Doughty were successful in standing up to the Company, but its powers were still extensive. Like their 15th-century predecessors in the Mercers' Guild, searchers were appointed from within the membership and had the power to enter any shop, cellar or warehouse of any member or of any other merchant in York or its suburbs and 'to make searche as well of all false and corrupte waires, and marchandize, as also of all weightes and metwandes'. The 1603 ordinances empowered the sergeant to arrest any offenders and take them to the prison on Ouse Bridge, but in practice punishment was a monetary fine, like that for John Wood who was presented in 1678 'for 4 ½lb weights wanting each 2 ounces'.

In order to check whether traders were using the correct weights, the searchers took the national standard weights and measures with them. The Company bought 'a pare of paun scales and small exchequer weights from a pound to a dram' at a cost of 9s. but there were complaints in 1706 that the standard weights were 'worn light and wrong'. The court asked the Governor 'to write to London for a new sett according to the standard, which his worship promised to doe'.

The changing face of the Company was reflected in its petition to Parliament for a bill allowing its officers to search all druggists and apothecary shops 'for the viewing, searching, and examining of all drugs, medicines, &c' as physicians in London were able to do. The petition was agreed at a 'secret committee' held at Mr Christopher Whitelock's house in February 1723. The following year another secret committee wanted to add another clause to the bill, this one 'praying leave for a boddy or two for dissection yearly', perhaps reflecting the interests of the growing number of apothecary members.

For Maud Sellers, writing in 1917, the Company's records of the Restoration and Georgian periods made

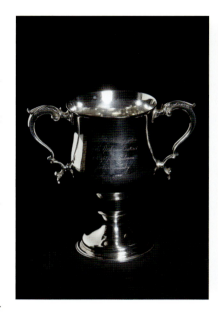
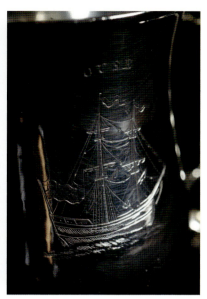

for 'sorry reading'. The 1581 charter marked, in her opinion, the start of a 'dreary story of retrogression', but the Company in fact kept closely to the terms of its charter. It continued to admit new members and to regulate its members' apprentices. No member was to keep a young man in his shop for more than six months without a formal apprenticeship, and although they came down hard on apprentices who started trading before they had served their full time, they also offered support on occasions, as they did to the apprentice whose master had left the city and 'takes noe care to provide for him nor doth in any kind imploy him'.

The Company maintained its interest in local transport, too, applying to the Commissioners of Trustees of the River Ouse for the 'heavy tonnage now laid on all merchandize to be entirely taken off', and campaigning for improvements like the construction of the Ouse lock at Naburn in 1757 and the canalisation of the Foss between 1793 and 1805. Improvements in the roads made trade easier, and there was some revival of trade in the second half of the 18th century, when the city staiths were once again busy with cargoes for a while. In 1769–71, a group of York Merchants invested in a 'New Contract', raising the money to build a fleet of six brigantines, 'without shifting bottoms', which enabled them to by-pass Hull and trade directly with London. A silver cup engraved with a picture of one of the fleet and presented by the proprietors to Capt. John Coulman 'for his Assiduity' is still in the possession of the Company.

Two-handled silver cup engraved with a ship, 'Ouse', and the words 'The Gift of the Proprietors of the new Contract to Capt. John Coulman for his Assiduity. May 1777.'

Nor were the aims of charity, fraternity and religion that had linked the original fraternity to the Mercers' Guild forgotten. The Company continued to administer the hospital, to provide poor relief, to worship in the chapel and to offer members support in times of need just as the owners of the Hall had always done. Poor women, usually widows, were able to petition for places in the hospital as they became available, and unsuccessful candidates were given relief from the poor box. Members appear to have paid an annual subsidy of 10d. 'for every free brother and sister' which was for 'brotherhood and poore'. Members were still referred to as brethren, in an echo of the Company's roots in the religious fraternity, and they still supported each other when required, although the support was usually financial. The Governor in 1691 was reimbursed by the wardens for the 17s. 6d. he paid towards the burial of Abraham Askwith, and the court held in September 1708 agreed to provide 40s. towards the funeral costs of Mrs Hart, who 'being at the point of death' had 'humbly' begged for a contribution so that she could be buried next to her husband. Presumably a member of the Company, Mrs Hart had once run the Cloth Hall on Ouse Bridge, and may have been the same Mrs Ann Hart who in 1681 was given £10 from the Company's stock 'towards the redemption of her sonne John Hart, now a slave in Algeir'. The unfortunate Mrs Hart had to raise a further £30 herself before the money would be handed over, and to satisfy the Company 'that there is certaine hope and probability of geting him released thereby', and, they added cautiously, 'that the money be not disposed of to any other end.'

The list of benefactors now in the Undercroft shows that charitable giving was an important part of the Company culture, in spite of the rather cheese-paring attempts of the court in June 1693 to save costs by halving the special payments made to poor widows at Christmas, Easter and Whitsun. Michael Barstow's gift the following year may indeed have been a reaction to that decision. He gave a number of rents amounting to 40s. a year to be equally distributed among the poor widows in the hospital 'at the four most usuall feasts … or at the four quarterly court dayes'. Mrs Myers does not appear on the list of benefactors, but the minutes of 1691 record that she bequeathed £50 to the Company which was to be loaned out at a rate of 5%, the interest from which was to be paid to two poor widows whose husbands had been free of the Company. Members who had fallen on hard times were also supported, as those belonging to the 14th-century fraternity had been. John Hall, 'a poor brother', was paid 12d. a week in 1746, at the discretion of the wardens, and only until the following Michaelmas court.

Much of the Company's business in the 17th and 18th centuries, in fact, was concerned with the administration of various loans to help young men start trading. William Wooller left £100 to be lent to 'two young merchants' for three years without interest, while William Hart gave £600 to be lent to 12 young merchants for two years, also without interest (*see p.35*). The men lent £50 apiece under the terms of Wooller's grant were noted as being 'Merchant Adventurers of England' and therefore involved in overseas trade, but the beneficiaries of Hart's gift were not specified in the same way. His money was lent in 1678 to eight merchants, two mercers and two grocers. Members had to be found to stand surety for

The Company awarded £10 to Mrs Hart to help her release her son who was being held as a slave in Algiers.

all loans, and the wardens chased up any outstanding repayments. On occasion, the Company even offered mortgages. Having already borrowed £50 Joseph Scott approached the court in 1693 for a further loan of £100. The court agreed to lend £150 at 5 per cent interest, 'provided he give land securely for the same in such manner as Counsell shall approve & direct'. The support of young entrepreneurs is another tradition that continues to this day.

Although there is little detail in the minute books, the Company maintained a religious side as well as a commercial one. Thomas Herbert, who kept Charles I company the night before his execution, died in 1644 and left £30 'to the end there shall be a sermon preached every Michaelmas Court viz.: twenty shillings to the parson, ten shillings to the poor women; if no sermon, the whole to be divided amongst the poor women.' Jane Stainton (d.1692) also bequeathed money for a sermon to be preached at All Saints Pavement every year on 30 January, the anniversary of the execution of Charles I, to put hearers 'in mind of their latter end'. There were sermons before some courts, and members who absented themselves or turned up late were fined. A chaplain was paid to take services in the Chapel and to be a reader to the poor women in the hospital.

The association with St Crux Church that dated back to the mid-14th century lasted until the church was demolished in the 19th century, but the Company was jealous of its right of appointment. When Ruben Buskill was appointed 'clark to the merchants for their chappell and likewise reader to the poor hospitall women by two different erection of hands' in 1708, the court noted that 'no clark of Crux Church shall have any rights or claime to be reader to the hospitall women, or clerk to our chapel, but by the choise of this fellowship'. In 1688 the Governor reported that he had been approached by several French Protestants living in York, who 'doo desire leave to have the use of our Chapel for a minister to preach to them in the French tongue'. The court agreed 'provided noe damage be done thereby to the chappell'.

As mentioned earlier, the hospital was still very much the Company's responsibility, and a good many of the entries in the minute books are concerned with gifts from the poor box to poor women, and occasionally to men. In 1678 Ann Hoggard, 'the poor

woman that makes clean the Hall', was given 2s. 6d. 'in relief out of the poore box'. The following year she was paid for her expenses in 'besomes, rubbers and skuttles', but by 1680 she was clearly unwell. When the poor women were awarded 10s. from the poor box, the court specified 'and one shilling particularly to An Hoggard being sick'. Hard-headed the merchants may have been, but they were not as mean-spirited as Maud Sellers suggested. Later that year, they decided to give Ann 2s. '& 6d a week for as long as she lives and continues soo weak'. When the hospital was flooded in 1681, the women were given an extra 3s. each, 'their goods and fuell having bin much damaged by the late high water'

In 1735 the Governor reported that he had received complaints about the behaviour of some of the women in the hospital and proposed not only a scheme 'for the better regulation' of the hospital but also for an infirmary to be provided in case of sickness.

Detail of view of Pavement with St Crux Church, right, and the Parish and Guild Church of All Saints, centre, both churches with which the Company has always had a close relationship. St Crux was demolished in 1886/7. (Artist unknown, early 19th century).

The board on the pillar reads:

> ...happened soon after the date of his Will dated Nov.9th 1699, gave to this Church ...ordered by her Sister Margaret Stainton for a Sermon every 30th of Jan.y and 3.s and 30.s yearly for educating 6 Poor Girls of the age of 6 or 7 till they be 11 or 12 years old all payable out of the House in Coppergate now inhabited by Samuel Blyth. NB. The Money is Annually paid by the Governor of the Merchants Company.

The Guild Church of All Saints Pavement. The board recording the Jane Stainton bequest is on the pillar on the right.

A dispensary was set up in the Hall in 1788 (*see box, p. 73*) and the Company also supported a soup kitchen for the poor and a school for six poor children under the terms of Jane Stainton's bequest.

If the Company continued the traditions of charity and religion that dated back to the 14th century, the social aspects of membership appear to have been less obvious during this period. The Venison Feasts lapsed during the 17th century, although there was an attempt to revive them in 1690 when the Governor asked the wardens 'to search the companys book to see how the last feast was managed'. The Hall was certainly used for feasting at the time, but these appear to have been private affairs and not part of the

Company's activities. Indeed, the minutes of a court held in March 1695 reported disapprovingly that

> *Upon the view of our Hall it appears that some damage hath been done to the Tables, Formes, Benches, Windows and other things by such as have had liberty to Feast therein, the Company therefore doe desire the Governor that if his worship think fit to give leave to anybody to use the same hereafter he will be pleased to take a note under their hands to repair what Damages shall be done thereby.*

Three years later, when Sheriff Radley had to make good the damages done to the Hall after his feast, it was

John Stow

There are far fewer portraits from the 18th century than there are for the two centuries either side, so it was good that the portrait of a leading member of the Company from this period was able to be purchased at auction. The sitter is John Stow, Governor for three years from 1773 to 1775. His name can be seen on one of the benefaction boards in the Chapel. He was apprenticed to Henry Bower, mercer and Merchant Adventurer, in 1742, when he was also made free of the city. Like so many Merchants he was fully involved in the life of the city, serving as Chamberlain in 1748/9, and then as Sheriff in 1763. He died in 1775 and is buried in the chancel of St Helen's Church, as is his wife, Catherine. Their fine neo-classical memorial tablet can still be seen. The parish register describes him as 'the most eminent silk mercer in York'. Stow's son, John, followed in his father's footsteps as a silk mercer and Merchant Adventurer. In the portrait Stow is shown wearing a smart outfit of mushroom-coloured silk. His wife's portrait, hanging alongside, shows her fashionably dressed in a silk gown. When offered for sale initially the portraits were optimistically attributed to Wright of Derby. That attribution is not credible, but so far the artist who painted these quite accomplished likenesses has not been identified, though the name of Christopher Steele (1733–68) has been suggested.

The Great Hall continues to be used for social events today.

decided that anyone wanting to use the Hall for feasts would have to pay either 20s. if they were a member, or 40s. if not. The charges were later raised to 30s. for brethren and £3 for non-members, and the court was clearly considering the matter seriously. They sent for workmen in 1698 and asked 'what the charge of putting up a chimney there and making a large firestead would bee, in order to make our Hall more commodious for feasting and to prevent any mischeife being done by making fires against the wall in the court yard'. Today it is still possible to hire the Hall for special occasions, albeit at a rather greater cost, and the Company faces a similar dilemma of wanting to make it accessible while ensuring that no damage is done. Letting out the Great Hall has always been a risky business, as the Company discovered in 1738 when members voted to make the city sheriffs pay for damage caused when 'entertaining their company'.

From the late 16th century onwards the Great Hall above the hospital took on an increasingly public role. Poverty and vagrancy were major issues in early modern York as elsewhere and the civic authorities attempted to deal with the influx of the poor and to crush any threat of disorder by severely restricting their movements. A distinction was made between the deserving poor and those who were 'ydle and vagrant'. The former were allowed to beg or put to work, while those stigmatised as shiftless and lazy risked severe punishment if they remained. A vagrant caught in the city might be tied to a cart and whipped through the streets before being literally thrown outside the walls. With the exception of the last leg out to Walmgate Bar, the route these brutal processions took followed that taken by the pageant wagons when the mystery plays were performed in the streets of York.

Well into the 17th century the poor were grouped together for 'viewings' to decide their fate. These viewings took place in the Guildhall and in the Merchant Adventurers' Hall, then known as Trinity Hall, although the Hall does not seem to have been used as a workhouse in the way St Anthony's Hall was. Nonetheless, the presence of large numbers of people must have had an impact on the way the Hall was used, and there was an increasing trend towards the use of smaller, more private, rooms for meetings (*see Chapter 5*).

In the late 16th century a room was constructed at the back of the Great Hall. Now known as the Committee Room, it seems to have been originally intended to store cloth. The 1603 ordinances enacted 'that no brother of this fellowshipp shall herafter go to se or buye anie cloth brought to this cittye to be sold in no place but in our hall'. Clearly the Hall was intended as a centre of trade at this point, but once the Merchant Adventurers of England had set up a separate residence in the city, the Cloth Hall moved to Ouse Bridge, and the Great Hall was put to increasingly public use. It was still used for meetings and formal admissions to the Company, as well as the viewings of the poor and private feasts, but the sheer size of the Hall made it invaluable for other purposes. The Deputy Governor told the court in April 1685 that 'the occasion of sumoning them to meet at this time was to let them know that some stage players being come to Towne did desire to take our Hall for a play house for which they were willing to pay ten shillings a weeke and to leave all things as they found them.' There was some debate, but sadly the vote was 'carried in the negative.' Perhaps plays were considered too frivolous a pursuit for a hall more normally used for the solemn business of the swearing of oaths.

As membership dwindled in the 18th century, the Hall's enormous size became impractical, and it was divided by a wooden partition. In spite of the new sash windows, installed in the 1730s, the rooms must have made unwelcoming meeting places, and nearby inns or the fashionable coffee houses often offered more appealing venues. After the opening formalities of court in 1739, the members adjourned to Hill's coffee house, where they continued to discuss Company business in warmth and comfort.

Opposite: The scales on display in front of the Governor's Stall in the Great Hall.

THE BEADLE

The account roll of 1368 notes that 2d. was paid to a man sent to invite the members of the guild to attend the funeral of one of their brethren, one of the Beadle's most important tasks in the pre-Reformation period. By 1603, the Beadle was referred to as the Sergeant, and was elected with the powers to arrest either the body or the goods of any person or persons inhabiting within the City of York for offences committed against the acts of the Company. Under the Company's authority, he could convey such malefactors to the prison upon Ouse Bridge and hand them in for safe keeping. In 1775 the post was held by John Bilton and the title was changed back to Beadle. The Beadle was issued a staff of office, often and incorrectly termed a mace, and was required to protect the Governor and to maintain discipline, particularly amongst the apprentices. Today the Beadle continues to fulfil this role on ceremonial occasions when he precedes the Governor carrying his ceremonial staff.

Above: Beadle Bruce Wray leads the Governor's procession into the chapel.

Left: Thomas Henry 'John' Fletcher, Beadle 1901–13.

Survival and Recovery:
1800–1939

CHAPTER 3

Survival and Recovery:

1800–1939

The Company's fortunes were at a nadir as it entered the 19th century. While other northern cities were booming, York remained very much a market town, a centre of exchange for goods and services in the region as it had always been, but largely bypassed by the industrialisation that had transformed the towns of the West Riding, and its reputation as a great trading city lost.

The Company continued its vigorous defence of what it saw as the monopoly granted by Elizabeth I, insisting that all shopkeepers dealing in imported goods had to become members, but the policy was counter-productive in the end, driving traders out of the import trade rather than convincing them to join. When the Company turned its attention to York's chemists, or druggists, its legal assault backfired. John Harwood, a druggist in Petergate, refused to acknowledge the monopoly and successfully defended himself against the Company when it took him to court. The judge's ruling that the charter of 1581 did not, in fact, give the Company a monopoly on imported goods was a crushing blow. Not only did it have to accept that it had no authority over individual tradespeople wanting to sell imported goods, it also lost the £1,000 it had spent prosecuting the case. A local newspaper reported that the Harwood case, as it became known, had been 'fatal' to the Company's authority and hoped that 'the humbler shopkeepers of York may now follow their occupations in peace.'

A further blow was to come in 1835 when the Municipal Corporations Act swept away all guild restrictions on trade and industry, and with them

the Company's privileged position in York. The loss of the monopoly led to a decline in membership by apprenticeship, and to dwindling numbers generally. The minutes from the 19th century record very few admissions, and those new members that there were tended to be admitted by patrimony. Joseph Rowntree, when Governor in 1842, called for the Company to adopt a more open membership policy, and recommended initiatives such as a Commercial Reading Room and a Financial Exchange at the Hall. An exchange operated briefly between 1845 and 1847, and the minutes for 1846 note that the Hall was let 'for the purpose of an exchange room', but these schemes were only partially successful. The Governor in 1852 was still lamenting how numbers had fallen

Left: *Joseph Rowntree.*

60

over the past seven years, from nearly 100 to 48. Only 14 members were present on Charter Day 1861, plus the Beadle and Secretary, while just seven attended the same court in 1864.

The granting of honorary membership to influential figures in York became more common in the 19th century. George Hudson, the 'Railway King' and the man responsible for persuading George Stephenson to route the London railway line via York rather than Leeds, was offered the freedom of the Company in 1846, although there was a barbed note in his acceptance speech: 'Gentlemen, I am happy in becoming a member of this Ancient Company … I believe that this Company, if resuscitated, is yet able to render essential services to the state and benefit of the city.'

Clearly there was a big 'if' there as far as Hudson was concerned, and indeed the Company might well have decided to cut its losses at that point. Its fortunes at a low ebb and membership still declining, the Company nonetheless persevered and members today have good reason to be grateful to their 19th-

century predecessors. Thanks to them, the Hall and its priceless archives remain in Company ownership, and the traditions of charity and fraternity first promoted by the builders of the Hall in the 14th century endure to this day. The Herbert sermon continued to be preached as it had since the 17th century, and at the Head Court, as the Charter Day Court was known at the time, the previous Governor ceremonially handed over custody of the Company's 1581 charter in a mahogany box, together with the Company's seal, the silver cup, the brass yard wand and a wooden hammer. Today these historic items are kept safely under lock and key, but at the time they represented the continuity of the Company's rituals.

The Venison Feasts which had enjoyed a brief revival at the end of the 17th century had long died out, but in the middle of the 19th century the Head Court was usually marked by a breakfast. As the Company's influence declined, its descriptions became more grandiose. The Great Hall was now referred to as the State Room. Before the 1854 court, the Company

Previous pages: The north-west elevation showing the original timbers and the only remaining four-light mullion still in use.

Below: The Thomas Herbert sermon is preached in the Chapel before the Michaelmas Court in 1910.

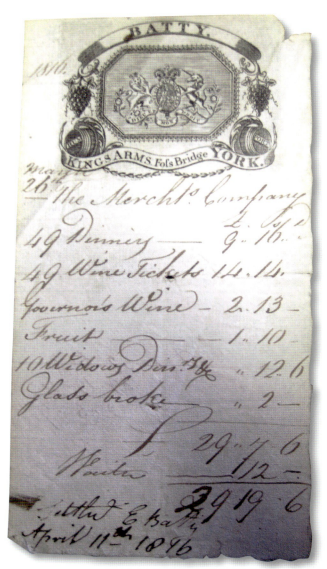

Far left: Bill for a dinner on March 26 1817, for 49 people; the bill includes charges for broken glass, candles, waiting and dinners for ten widows, presumably inmates of the hospital.

Left: Cartoon by Sir Frank Lockwood. Lockwood was MP for York and a member of the Company.

the entertainment, and with the joyousness and good humour which pervaded the proceedings of the evening throughout. The ancient loving cup was passed round to the Queen's Health as usual, between the courses.' Not all the spreads were quite as lavish. The Head Court in 1850 ended more frugally with the Governor inviting the court 'to partake of a Glass of wine and a Biscuit in the Hall before the members separated'.

Stripped of its privileges, the Company nonetheless continued to take an interest in commercial issues and petitioned Parliament regularly on issues relating to trade and transport, both of which were transformed during the 19th century. Ouse Bridge was rebuilt in the second decade of the century, but the real change came with the arrival of the railways after 1840, revolutionising communications and the economy of York itself. The Company acted as a pressure group for projects such as the Wakefield–Ferrybridge canal in 1828, the York–Scarborough railway (1837–44) and Foss Navigation Bill of 1852. In 1877 a project for the improvement of navigation on the Ouse was discussed in court, with members in agreement that 'it is of the utmost importance to the Mercantile and general interests of the City that the Navigable

'which included several of the principal Citizens of York' sat down to 'a most splendid Breakfast in the State Room'. Wine was served 'to drink the Health of our most gracious Queen'. These breakfasts, always described as 'splendid' or 'sumptuous' or 'excellent', were catered for by various nearby inns and were a regular feature until they appear to have died out in the 1860s. A dinner, rather than a breakfast, was provided after the Michaelmas Court in 1852. This, too, was served in the 'State Room' and as well as members the Lord Mayor and a 'large party of influential clergymen and tradesmen' were present. After the usual toasts, 'the hilarity of the evening was maintained until a reasonable hour when the company separated, highly delighted with the exceeding hospitable character of capabilities of the River Ouse should be developed to the utmost possible extent.' The Company heard 'with satisfaction' about the proposed widening of Naburn Lock in 1879, a work they considered 'to be one of paramount importance to the mercantile advance and prosperity of the City', but they were adamantly opposed to the building of a Hull–Lincoln railway with its bridges that would affect the navigability of the Ouse, and protested vigorously against the railway rates and charges bill of 1891.

The second half of the 19th century, in fact, saw the Company attempting to reinvent itself as a commercial force in the city. A local newspaper reported in 1879 that the Company had enjoyed 'a very pleasant evening at Harker's Hotel' where 'many good wishes were expressed for the future prosperity of the company which will now shortly take once more an active part in promoting and developing the trade and commerce of this city of which in former times it was the principal representative.' The Company deliberately attempted to strengthen its position and influence in the city by attracting as many new members 'not being entitled to be admitted … by patrimony or servitude as may be willing to take up their freedom on payment of the sum of £5.'

The railway and confectionery industries were booming in York in the 1870s, and the Company set out to attract the leading businessmen of the city, men like Sir Joseph Terry who brought a new energy to the Company and who combined commercial acumen with philanthropic interests. In 1881 the freedom of the Company was presented to George Leeman, who had been a powerful figure in the railway world since the downfall of his rival Hudson. The honorary membership testified to the members' sense of Leeman's 'lengthened services to the mercantile and other interests of this City' and Leeman's reply that it was 'an honour of no mean worth' perhaps reflects the extent to which the Company had succeeded in turning its fortunes around. Indeed, the Company ended the century on a high note, with the founding of the Chamber of Commerce in York. The Chamber's first meeting was held in the Hall on 26 January 1897.

The railway sidings in 1860. York's first railway station was built within the city walls.

Although members were clearly conscious of their mercantile history, most of the 19th-century minutes nonetheless give the impression that for many the Company functioned primarily as a 'gentlemen's club'. Whenever a member died, fulsome letters of sympathy and their replies were carefully copied into the minutes. In keeping with the spirit of the times, when all things medieval were wildly popular, the members became increasingly interested in their own collections and in what would today be called the heritage value of the Hall. This was partly inspired by the restoration work which gradually re-exposed the medieval timber framing as the layers of 17th- and 18th-century plaster were removed, and by the rediscovery of the Company's Register and Cartulary – listing its charters – which had fallen into private hands about 1730 and which were found in the Oakes library at Norton in 1890.

Another discovery brought a 'handsome gold signet ring', about 200 years old, back into the Company's possession. It was found by a labourer working on a house outside Walmgate Bar in 1888 and identified by Canon James Raine, an honorary member, as having been worn by previous Governors of the Company in an official capacity because, as he explained, 'no private member had the right to use the corporate arms'. Purchased by John Francis Taylor, a past Governor, the ring was presented to the Company and is still worn by the Governor at Charter Day, and at other times is on display in the Governor's Parlour.

Taylor also gave the Company the portrait of Queen Henrietta Maria that hangs in the Great Hall today (*see p.45*). A number of other paintings were given to the Company at this time, along with drawings, old letters, a silver snuff box, and a policy of fire insurance dating to 1793 taken out by James Saunders, who had been an apothecary and Lord Mayor as well as a member of the Company. The Company's picture collection was becoming well known. It lent William Robinson's portrait to an exhibition of 'Yorkshire Worthies' in Leeds in 1868, and loaned a number of prints and pictures for an exhibition to mark the Prince of Wales's visit to the Royal Agricultural Show held in York in 1883.

In spite of its dilapidated state, the Hall was clearly of interest to visitors, whose numbers increased with the boom in tourism which followed the opening up

The Governor's ring.

of the railways. The first direct train between York and London ran in 1840, and by the 1850s there were 13 trains a day between the two cities. According to Maud Sellers, Charles Dickens visited repeatedly, drawn by the romanticism of the 'gloomy basement', and there were sufficient visitors to warrant the publication in 1893 of a 'little History' which could be sold by Mr and Mrs Fletcher, the caretakers, for 6d. a copy and which would 'entitle the Purchaser to admission to the Hall, Chapel, etc.'

With limited funds at its disposal, the Company did its best to maintain the Hall, although the restoration costs that followed the collapse of the ceiling in 1834, and the repairs to the windows and Chapel were considerable (*see Chapter 5*). The members made themselves more comfortable with a 'handsome new stove' placed in the Chapel prior to their meeting in 1852, 'which answers the desired end most satisfactorily', and in May 1865 some discussion took place 'as to the desirability of constructing a water closet for the use of the Hall in one of the rooms', although no more is mentioned about this in the minutes.

On a more day-to-day level, the Hall was maintained by the Hall-keeper, who appears to have combined the position with that of schoolmistress until 1875 when Mrs Tindall died and the trustees of the school decided to move premises. After that caretakers were employed. A Mrs Garnett was appointed to one of the vacancies in the Women's Hospital in lieu of being paid for cleaning the rooms after casual lettings. She and her husband were also to have the rooms previously occupied by Mrs Tindall, and to have their coal and gas free. There would be no pay for attendance at either

The Company's first honorary archivist, Dr Maud Sellers, on the steps of the Hall before the timbers were exposed.

Hall for £20 a year on condition that they kept the rooms clean. The arrangement had clearly suited the Company, which still provided for the education of six girls under the terms of Jane Stainton's will. When the school was moved, the Company had to make other arrangements. The property that funded Jane Stainton's bequest was sold in 1879, and the proceeds invested. This brought in a larger sum than the rents had done, and the Company decided to provide education for 12 children rather than six, and pay 7s. 6d. for each child instead of the 5s. that had been paid previously. At the same time, they doubled the fee to the minister who still preached a sermon in All Saints Pavement on 30 January, and the dole of bread to the poor was also doubled.

Other organisations made use of the Hall, which at this stage was still divided into two large rooms, with the Committee Room and the rooms on either side of the entrance, as well as the Undercroft. The York Union Lodge of Free Masons held their meetings in 'a certain public room known by the name of the Merchants Hall', as did the City & County Bank, who paid 26s. per meeting, and the Gas Company and Waterworks Company, who each paid 15s. for their meetings in 1867. Apparently taking the ceiling crashing down around them in their stride, Sunday schools were held in the Hall until 1888 when the Sunday School Committee wrote to say that they would be discontinuing their rent of rooms there. When the Jubilee celebrations were planned in 1887, the Hall seemed the obvious place to hold a tea party for schoolchildren. The Town Clerk wrote asking permission, which the Company granted 'on condition that care be taken to have the children kept under proper control'. The wonderfully named Society for the Encouragement of Faithful Female Servants met in the Hall in 1828, while later in the century the Company considered an application from the University Extension Committee to rent the Hall for one night a week for a course of 10 or 12 lectures to be given to the 'operative classes'.

Penny Bank or Sunday schools or Company meetings, but they would get 2s. 6d. for each larger letting and 1s. for smaller ones, 'to include the lighting of fires and Gas and the usual attendance and the keeping of the two yards clean.' In 1881, Mrs Garnett was paid £5 a year 'for her trouble in taking care of and keeping clean the Hall and other rooms'.

The Hall was used on a regular basis, bringing the Company some much-needed income in lieu of admission fees. There was a school in the Hall for some 50 years, until the death of the schoolmistress in 1875, at which point the trustees of Dorothy Wilson's charities decided to remove it to one of the schools in St Denys's Parish. For the previous 20 years the school had been known as the Foss Bridge school, and was allowed to use rooms in the

While various meetings and classes took place upstairs, the Undercroft was still functioning as a hospital. A plan drawn up in 1814 clearly shows rooms set aside for women's bedrooms and apartments, separated from those for the male inmates. There were in addition two large spaces, one of which was

THE BANNERS

The colourful banners in the Undercroft display the arms of the various medieval guilds of York. They were painted for the 1909 York Pageant. The artist who painted most of them was a Company member, Walter Winterton, and his portrait, painted by his son, hangs in the Hall.

In Edwardian England there was a great interest in historical pageants, and rivalry between cities in staging them. The six-day York event took place in the Museum Gardens with an experienced director, Louis Parker, as 'Master of the York Pageant'.

The banners were brought to the Hall by Alderman Foster during his year as Governor, an event reported by *The Yorkshire Herald* in 1910:

These banners were produced with infinite care under the direction of Mr. T.P. Cooper, who devoted an immense amount of research to secure accuracy and completeness. They were painted by some of the most skilful workmen

Above: *Some of the cast of the 1909 York Pageant assembled in the Museum Gardens.*

in York, and were universally admired for their brilliant colouring. Alderman Foster secured them at the sale of Pageant properties, and rightly thinking that there could be no more appropriate home for them than the historic home of the Merchant Adventurers, he has had them hung in the old Hall.

The 20 banners represent the arms of the Ancient Guilds of the city, as follows: Girdlers, Glaziers, Ropers, Grocers, Cordwainers, Merchant Adventurers, Masons, Cloth Workers, Millers, Goldsmiths, Curriers, Pewterers, Skinners, Tallow Chandlers, Dyers, Vintners, Merchant Taylors, Weavers, Tanners and Feltmakers.

Left: *Today the banners are displayed in the Undercroft.*

Above: *The Merchant Adventurers' pageant banner.*

Top: *The banners were painted by Company member Walter Winterton, second from right, assisted by his son Edgar, right, for the 1909 York Pageant.*

described as a 'public' hall. These appear to have been used for storage. One of the Company's tenants, Mr Lunn, was allowed to place empty casks underneath the Hall in 1846, as long as the passageway was not obstructed, and later in the century Messrs. Young & Co. rented the 'vaults' until their tenancy expired in 1892. Once they had vacated the premises, the Company decided to re-let the space and made arrangements to take down the old coal boxes in the cellar, whitewash the walls and relay the floor with bricks – as long as the cost was not more than £5.

It is difficult to work out exactly how the Undercroft was used at this stage. The Company continued to administer the hospital, and applicants for places were interviewed whenever a vacancy arose. Candidates appeared in person, and the committee voted as to who should be appointed. When Mrs Hall died in 1853, her place was given to Mrs Taylor, a merchant's widow, 'having the greatest number of scrawls'. There

were places for both men and women in the hospital in the 19th century, but it is not clear how many of the 'hospitallers' actually lived there. A transcript of the 1825 report of the Charity Commissioners made in 1887 recorded that the 'building consists of two large rooms under the Company's Hall in Fossgate, one of them being divided into sitting and sleeping rooms for five poor men and the others in the like manner for five poor women.'

Clearly some inmates did live in the hospital. Indeed, the minutes of 1858 record that the painting and other repairs of the Hall and almshouses had been completed and that 'all the Hospitallers but one were residing on the premises'. In 1861 the committee elected John Waineford unanimously for one of the vacant positions in the men's hospital. The second went to a vote and was awarded to James Gray 'who promised to reside in the Hospital'. A printed notice of 1893 postponing the service in the Chapel 'owing to serious illness in one of

Tea party held in the partitioned Great Hall after the Michaelmas Court in 1910.

the Rooms connected with the Merchants' Hall' suggests that the hospital was still occupied, but when Thomas Garnett and his wife, once caretakers of the Hall, were unable to work due to 'extreme age and infirmity' they were found a room in St Martin's Coney St parish rather than in the hospital itself. They continued to receive their weekly allowance as hospitallers, and when they both died in 1894 two vacancies were created in spite of the fact that they had been living out.

Membership had reached its lowest point in 1875, when the Company had only 10 members. However, by 1900, when Sir Joseph Sykes Rymer was Governor, the number had increased to more than 40. Sir Joseph, coincidentally, was the great-grandfather of David Rymer (Governor 1989–90), who at the time of writing was the longest serving member of the Company, having joined in April 1957. When objecting to the Charity Commissioners' proposal in 1910 that they should take over the management of its charities, the Company noted that while it only had 45 members, its numbers were continuing to grow. The membership might be small, but it was influential, including two MPs, six ex-Lord Mayors, four ex-sheriffs, the Town Clerk, several members of the city council, many leading merchants and 15 Justices of the Peace. Efforts were being made to attract new members, with 16 admissions in 1910. Later minutes show new members being admitted on a regular basis, although not in any great numbers. Indeed, a certain exclusivity may have been part of the Company's appeal. A merchant, a stockbroker and a banker were admitted by purchase in 1925, while admissions in 1929, when J. Bowes Morrell was

Restoration work in the Great Hall in 1937.

Governor, included Oliver Sheldon, Cuthbert Morrell, Christopher John Rowntree and Peter Rowntree. A number of families like the Herberts, the Rowntrees, the Terrys, the Rymers and the Barstows have been associated with the Company over the generations, in a tradition that is often a point of pride.

The early 20th-century minutes are often cursory compared to those of earlier centuries. Instead, the concerns of members are reflected in the newspaper cuttings that are pasted into the minute books. Some of these, such as accounts of funerals, the 1935 Silver Jubilee service in the Minster, or the Proclamation of Edward VIII, have references to the Company of Merchant Adventurers underlined in red, but a good many are detailed reports of the Herbert sermon and the meetings that followed. The sermons are particularly interesting examples of how history is rewritten in the light of contemporary attitudes. In the aftermath of the First World War, the xenophobia of the British was reflected in the 1928 Herbert sermon, which was given by the Dean of York, Lionel Ford, who urged the Company to remember the ideals of their predecessors 'in the dark days of the 14th and 15th centuries when England was under the heel of the German Hanseatic League'. Their aim, the Dean claimed, had been 'to free England' from the League and by working together, the merchants 'beat the Hanseatic League and by August 4 1598 the Germans were turned out of England.'

The Stainton sermon in 1930 was preached by Rev. A.A.R. Gill, who took a romantic approach to the history of the Merchant Adventurers, exhorting the congregation to think of how:

Their forefathers in days of yore pulled out across the deep on that life of adventure which would always redound to their undying fame. They were not men cringing behind their founders, but took their lives in their hands, voyaged in wretched boats across the uncharted seas to sell goods in hostile and foreign countries.

How different would the history of England have been if it had not turned to the adventuring spirit of days gone by. Who was the greater? The merchant who suffered and helped to build up, as he undoubtedly did, a lasting civic organisation or the soldiers whose ravaging left behind nothing but waste?

A remarkable woman: Dr Maud Sellers (1861–1939)

Honorary Curator, archivist and prime mover in the restoration of the Merchants' Hall

The famous historian, A.J.P. Taylor, wrote in his autobiography in 1983 that he had 'learnt more history from Maud Sellars (sic) at the Merchant Adventurers' Hall in York than I did from all my tutors in Oxford'. Her guided tours were a delight to the visitor of whatever age or learning. H.V. Morton, the travel writer, notes in *The Call of England* (first published in 1928) that when visitors paid their sixpence for a ticket, a white-haired woman would appear to conduct them round the Hall. 'Before she has spoken three words you know that she is no ordinary curator … When she refers to the Merchant Adventurers of York she says "we" not "they" … with considerable pride as though she were a Merchant Adventurer! As a matter of fact she is! She is the only woman Merchant Adventurer in the world and the only woman who is a full liveried member of a city company … known in York as "Dr Maud".'

Maud Sellers came from obscure origins, but her intellect led her to Cambridge, where she graduated from Newnham College, Cambridge, and in 1907 she was awarded an Honorary Doctorate of Literature by Dublin University in recognition of her services to English economic history. She gained a handful of prestigious travelling scholarships, and when staying in York discovered at the offices of Mr Wilkinson, Solicitor and Secretary of the Company, the papers of the Eastland Company and the rich seam of the Merchants' archive in the Hall. She devoted the best part of the rest of her life to bringing these records and the Hall itself into the public eye.

When she came to the Hall, the Company consisted of some 25 members supporting a decayed building. The force of her enthusiasm and personality inspired successive governors and members to make liberal donations towards the restoration of the Hall. She was responsible for the restoration of the Undercroft, which involved clearing away several walls and exposing to view a beautiful Undercroft upheld by great pillars of solid oak trunks. Her scholarly researches were variously published by the Royal Historical Society and the Camden and Surtees Societies. She also made many valuable contributions to the Victoria County History. She was admitted to honorary membership of the Company in 1913, the first woman Merchant Adventurer for nearly 400 years, and was appointed Honorary Curator in 1918 (and Honorary Archivist to the city of York in 1923 for similar work on the medieval records).

When she died in Bournemouth on 14 June 1939, aged 78, the Company had over 70 members and the restoration work on the Hall was almost complete.

Left: A page from Maud Seller's working papers showing biographical notes of apprentices in 17th-century York.

The minutes of the early 20th century are dominated by concerns about the fabric of the Hall and about its exterior. At the beginning of the century, the only access to the Hall was from Fossgate, but when Piccadilly, a new street leading from Pavement, was created in 1913, the Company spied an opportunity for another entrance. For the next couple of years, discussions revolved around what to do with the land between the two entrances. In October 1915, it approached the Corporation with a view to having the land laid out as a rest garden, although it seems this was not a universally popular idea. The minutes of April 1916 record that the scheme for laying out the land 'would not only make attractive an unsatisfactory space of land, but would give the Merchants Hall the pleasant and important position which is due to so very interesting and old a building'. The court recommended acquiring the ground between Piccadilly and the Hall to ensure 'the complete quietude which we associate with the precincts of historic buildings.' If that proved impossible, it was decided that 'the proposed Rest Garden will be the next best scheme.' The Company set about securing the adjoining land and removing the outbuildings that obscured 'the charming bit of old timber-work'. Small parcels of land were still being bought up in 1925, when the Piccadilly entrance was used for the first time.

Meanwhile, the Chapel and Undercroft were also in need of attention, and an appeal for subscriptions for the repair of the Hall was launched in 1921. The appeal seems to have been very successful, with major donations towards the cost of lighting and heating the Hall, enabling the Company to embark on an extensive repair programme that culminated in the dedication of the restored Undercroft and antechapel by the Archbishop of York, Cosmo Lang, in 1925. The Archbishop, who became an honorary member on the same occasion, preached the Herbert sermon and spoke about restoring the close union of business with charity, religion and human fellowship that had existed in the Middle Ages and which were so visibly expressed in the Hall.

There was still work to be done, however, as Maud Sellers pointed out. She suggested that the Company allow itself a year to recover from the restoration programme, 'but when that year expired there was in the Hall a sleeping beauty which pleaded

with them to allow the beauties of the Hall to be seen.' The Hall was officially scheduled as an ancient monument in 1935, but by 1937 it was reported as being in a 'serious state' with the cost of repairs set at £10,000. So bad was the condition of the Hall that the reception and Herbert sermon were cancelled that year. The Governor of the day decided against breaking with tradition by proposing an alternative venue: 'it would not be the same,' he thought, 'to hold the reception in a different building other than the Merchants Hall'. The repair programme attracted wide interest, with the *Yorkshire Post* declaring that the preservation of the Hall 'should be a national and not a private responsibility'.

Even in the run-up to war, the members of the Company kept its duty of care for the Hall at the forefront of their minds. A proposal to erect two air-raid protection shelters against the retaining wall on the Piccadilly side in 1939 met with a very lukewarm response. The minutes noted that while 'the Company were certainly public-spirited and realised the importance of the safety of the individual', they were nonetheless 'not anxious to have unsightly shelters on their open ground'. Still, the scheme seemed inevitable. The committee were left with the hope that if the shelters were erected, members would realise that the officers of the Company 'had done everything in their power to prevent it'.

The repair and maintenance of the Hall may have dominated much of court business in the first half of the 20th century, but the Company did not forget its other responsibilities. The proposal in 1910 that the Charity Commissioners should take over their charities was vigorously opposed. Two large rooms under the Great Hall were still being used 'for almshouse purposes' at that stage although it is still not entirely clear how many of the 'hospitallers' lived in the Hall. Each received a pension of 9s. a month, which was handed out by the wardens in the Great Hall. When vacancies arose, the Company advertised for applicants, sometimes specifying male or female, as in 1908. The response to the advertisements seems to have been high. In 1912 when two pensions were available, 15 people applied, while out of the 26 applicants in 1925, three were appointed: the widow of a bookseller, a decayed master tailor and a decayed carver and gilder. All applicants were interviewed by the Standing Committee and the

Members of the Company gather in the Undercroft after a service in 1932.

unsuccessful were given £5 from the Lancelot Foster Solatium Fund, which was set up in 1913. In the spirit of the original fraternity's charitable aims, Foster left £500 to fund gifts to 'aged poor women' residing in York 'being widows or daughters of decayed tradesmen' of the city who were unsuccessful applicants for the Company's pension.

The Hall continued to attract visitors. From 1 January 1914 admission cost 6d. per person, which included the price of a guidebook. The Hall-keeper was required 'to receive and attend with courtesy all visitors to the hall,' and received 1d. per guidebook sold 'in lieu of all fees and gratuities', with the remaining 5d. to be handed over to the Company. The extensive repair programme meant that there is little evidence of the Hall being used by other groups during this period, although in 1908 the York Miniature Rifle Club did ask permission to set up a rifle range in the Great Hall.

More noticeable is the interest in its own history that had also marked the Company's minutes in the later 19th century. In 1908 the Company agreed to a proposal for a selection of their records to be edited by Maud Sellers and published by the Surtees Society. This edition, which has formed the basis of most research on the Merchant Adventurers ever since, was eventually published in 1917, and in 1913 Dr Sellers herself was offered the freedom of the Company in recognition of her work (*see box, p.70*).

The beginning of the 20th century saw a growing interest in the rich historical heritage in York, and an extraordinary pageant took place in the Museum Gardens in 1909. A re-enactment of more than 2,000 years of history, it involved a cast of thousands, and a parade of the banners of the city's medieval guilds through the streets. The banners were presented to the Company in 1910, and are still displayed in the Undercroft (*see box, p.66*). The *York Herald* regularly reported on processions and meetings in the Hall, while the *Daily Mail* described the 1935 Michaelmas court in romantic terms: 'Candles burned at the altar, flickered by wafting currents of air down the corridors with their slanting oak-timbered walls and great open fireplaces where logs once burned.' The article, illustrated with

THE DISPENSARY

Between 1788 and 1808 the Merchant Adventurers' Hall played a key role in establishing one of the most important medical charities in the city. The York Dispensary was founded in 1788 to offer a free medical service to the poor. Staffed by local doctors and financially supported by the wealthy, it treated out-patients and home-patients and thus complemented the in-patient facilities at the York County Hospital.

The Dispensary was granted, at a rent of five guineas per week, the use of two rooms on the upper floor of the Hall: the kitchen, which was fitted up as the Apothecary's compounding room, and the Court of Assistants' meeting room, where the doctors met each week to examine patients.

The first Treasurer and the first Apothecary to the Dispensary were both Merchant Adventurers, which may explain why the Hall was chosen as the base for the charity. But despite its success – 17,000 patients were treated in the first 20 years – the accommodation was cramped and uncomfortable. The doctors had insufficient examination facilities and sick patients had to wait in an unheated room. So in 1808 the Dispensary moved to converted premises in St Andrewgate, and thereafter to other sites, until its free primary care service was made redundant by the new NHS in 1948.

a photograph of a crowded Undercroft, went on to describe the tea prepared in the Great Hall above, with 'cheese cakes and curd cakes on the table'. A 'woman caretaker' was quoted as saying that she had 'no doubt the first Merchant Adventurers would have had huge sides of beef instead'.

A suggestion in 1936 that a corner of the Hall should be used as a reference library 'for various issues of the history of the City' was quashed by Maud Sellers, who pointed out that the fabric of the building was still unsafe, but thanks to her work, the value of the Company's archive was more widely recognised. Tin boxes were purchased to store the medieval account rolls in 1913, and in later years important documents were returned to the Company. A 15th-century folio containing a list of apprentices, pageant masters and people to whom money had been lent by the Mercers' Guild came up for sale in 1936 and was bought for the Company by Past Governor H. Ernest Leetham for £20. The same year the minute books for 1693 to 1815, which record correspondence between York and Hamburg, were recovered at a sale by the Johnson brothers and also donated to the archives.

Maud Sellers died in 1939. Her death marked the end of an era for the Company, ending as it did a long association which led not only to her invaluable edition of the records in the Company archives but also made accessible the medieval history of the Hall that has become such an important part of its identity today. Change, of course, was coming anyway, as the Company, York and the rest of the world prepared for war.

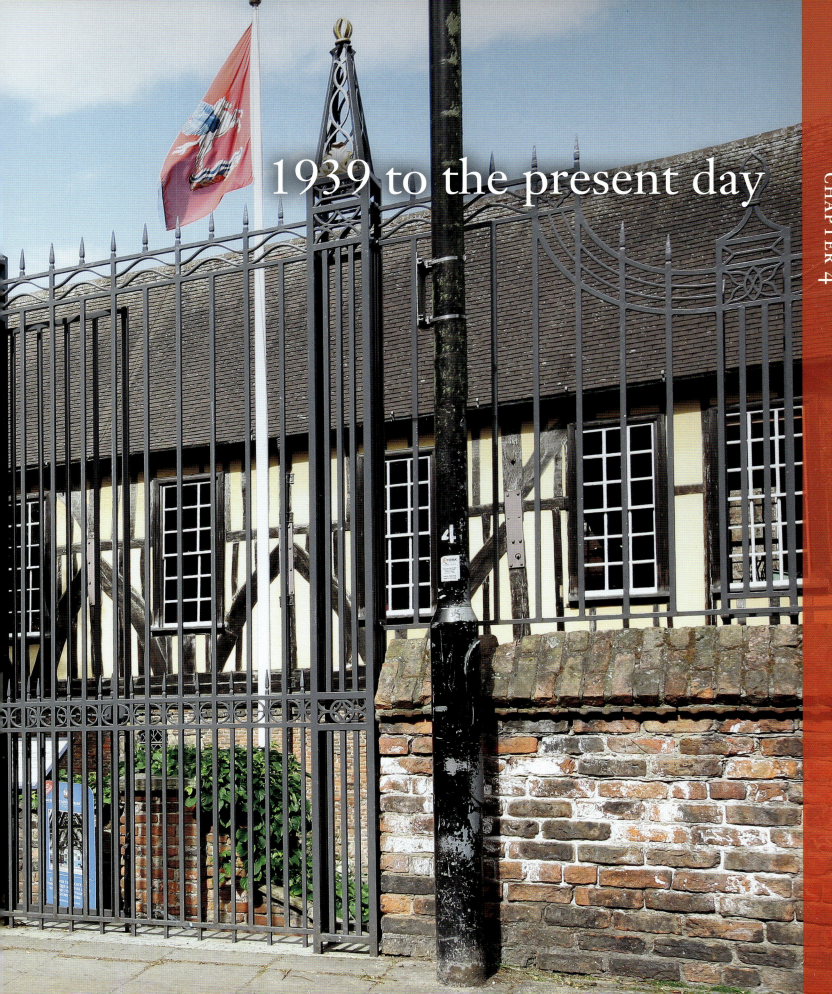

1939 to the present day

1939 to the present day

1939–45

The Company continued to meet throughout the War, but without the usual social gatherings, and discussions at the various courts were inevitably concerned with the national situation. Like everyone else, the Company prepared as best it could against the possibility of attack. The pictures were moved to the City Library, and sandbags were provided for the Hall, although they were so large that Past Governor Harold Bloor commented that 'no ordinary person could be expected to use them effectively'. Replacement bags were found and member Sydney Smith's offer to fill them was readily accepted. The Standing Committee cooperated with the Fossgate fire-fighting services, but a suggestion that air-raid shelters should be built against the retaining wall on the Piccadilly frontage was received without enthusiasm.

There were regular calls to use the Hall for war purposes. The Commandant of the Auxiliary Territorial Service (ATS) proposed that the Hall should be used as a canteen, but this was rejected. Unsuitability, heating costs and the difficulty of providing a blackout were the reasons given. The Countess of Sheffield's request for a room to sort library books before distribution to local military hospitals was also declined because the Company might then be overwhelmed with similar demands which could not be refused. However, the York Women's Voluntary Services (WVS) was allowed the use of the Hall to make camouflage netting, as it was a 'matter of National importance'. Because it took four days to bring the Hall to a comfortable temperature and blackout difficulties, this could only

be during the summer months. The WVS said 'they could not guarantee a Caretaker, but a capable woman would see that no damage was done'!

The Company endured the War years as it had other crises in its long history. With few resources available, it was a matter of 'hanging in' rather than any grand

Previous pages: *The Merchant Adventurers' Hall from Piccadilly.*

Below: *Members of the ATS march in Coney Street, April 1941.*

plans. Funds were low and recent building repairs costing £2,961 6s. 3d. had pushed the Company into an overdraft of £657 – secured by £1,000 of war stock. There was also a human cost to the War. Sworn in as a member in September 1943, Kenneth T.P. Terry was the first member to be killed in action in early 1944.

The Archbishop of York, Dr Cyril Garbett, a hugely influential figure, caught the mood on his election to membership of the Company in 1942, when he said: 'I have the greatest sympathy with the small merchant today, who is in danger of extinction … their successors in the modern world of adventure was the Merchant Navy which was doing splendid and vital work for the salvation of the nation.' He was doubtless strongly influenced by the heavy losses sustained during attacks on the Atlantic and Arctic convoys.

During the War years very little money was spent on the Hall, and by 1943 the seriousness of the financial situation could be avoided no longer. At the 1944 Charter Day court, a new Trust Deed was agreed. This marked another key turning point in the Company's history, legally defining as it did the Company of today and the way in which it operates (*see box, p.78*). As a result of the 1944 Trust Deed, the restoration and improvement of the Hall became, and is still, the primary duty of the Company – although perhaps not all the membership at that time (or since) fully appreciated that through the Court of Assistants they had now become liable for the building.

Annual voluntary donations were also introduced in 1944, with a contribution of 'something between £1 1s. 1d. and £5 5s. 5d.' At this time Company business was performed by the Standing Committee with the Court simply rubber-stamping their recommendations. Members complained that 'they do not get enough information about what is being done' and pressure was brought to hold four Courts each year instead of two. Furthermore the composition of the Standing Committee would be altered to allow greater membership participation on a rotating basis, and to improve transparency its minutes would be made available. It was hoped 'this would increase members' interest in company affairs'.

By Charter Day 1945 things were beginning to improve and the 400 visitors to the Hall over Easter that year generated £10 in admission fees.

1946 post-war renaissance
Despite everybody's best efforts during the War, problems remained, and when Oliver Sheldon was elected Governor at the 1946 Charter Day court, he initiated a series of far-reaching reforms.

Member Bernard Johnson was appointed Honorary Archivist and was asked to study the constitution of the Company and make recommendations for the resumption of a proper Court of Assistants. At the same time, member and architect J. Stuart Syme became Convener of the newly established Architects' Panel, and was charged 'as a matter of immediate urgency' to make a survey of the property and report on 'the repairs necessary to make good the arrears of war'. A three-year programme was to be prepared as a basis for raising future funds. A start was made on a complete inventory of the Company possessions and cleaning of the pictures. Oil paintings were hung in place of the photographs of past Governors.

A special court in May 1946 amended the rules for the intake of members and agreed that the archives

The Master of the Worshipful Company of Mercers, Captain H.K. Totton RN, presents two silver gilt cups to Governor Christopher Rowntree after being sworn in as an honorary member at the Special Court of 19 June 1952.

The Trust Deed of 1944

The Company's archives reveal the extent of the problems faced by the Company during the Second World War. Younger members were serving in the armed forces and others were involved in essential war work. The active membership was therefore reduced in number at a time when the condition of the Hall was causing concern and money was tight.

As early as 1937 *The Yorkshire Post* had carried a report referring to the Hall being in a serious state and requiring expenditure of £10,000 for its restoration. Later in the year the newspaper had reported that an infestation of death-watch beetle had been found. The Company's financial position is illustrated by a minute of a meeting of the standing committee of the Court of Assistants held on 26 May 1943. While the committee decided to advertise for pensioners, it was considered that 'the funds of the Company were so low that they would hardly warrant the payment of additional pensions.' With these challenges to be met, the Company had to act to safeguard its finances and to secure the official recognition of its status as a charity trustee. Although a formal document was needed in order to obtain the tax benefits available to charities, the Trust Deed of 5 April 1944 also served two other important purposes.

The first of these was to record what was described in the Deed as 'the settled practice of the Company'. In its introductory clauses the Deed referred to the Company's ownership of the Hall and Chapel, and the uses to which these had been put. It referred also to the fact that the income arising from the Company's properties in Fossgate and from its other trust investments, together with members' donations, had been applied in maintaining the Hall and Chapel and providing 'pensions for decayed tradesman of the said City (York)'. The second purpose was to make a formal declaration that the Company would in future apply that income and those donations for the maintenance and repair of the Hall and Chapel and the payment of pensions to decayed tradesmen of the city of York or its suburbs, or for the benefit of poor and deserving persons of the said city.

Phrases such as 'decayed tradesmen' and 'poor and deserving persons' are now seen as being archaic and member David Blackburn therefore approached the Charity Commission on behalf of the Company and successfully applied for a scheme to modernise the language used to describe the classes of beneficiary. At the same time the Commission agreed to redefine the area of benefit so as to reflect the current boundary of the City of York which extends much further than was the case in 1944. The scheme has recently been sealed and provides for 'the payment of pensions to persons who have been engaged in trade in the area of benefit, and the dependants of such persons, who are in need because of age, illness or other infirmity, or the relief of financial hardship among persons resident in the area of benefit by such means as the trustee thinks fit'.

The Company, having achieved this updating, looks forward to pursuing its duties as a charity trustee under the 1944 Deed as altered by the scheme.

of the Company should be put under the charge of the Honorary Archivist and be deposited at the Bank. This court also agreed that the Master of the Worshipful Company of Mercers of London should be invited each year to become an honorary member to revive the association of the two companies which had been so close in the 15th and 16th centuries. This tradition has continued ever since.

A similar tradition of reciprocal hospitality was developed with the other York guilds although it was felt inappropriate to revive the Venison Feast. As the Governor said, 'The times are against such convivial festivities'. Instead the Court, Officers and guests of the Company were entertained to dinner at the Station Hotel after the Charter Day Court, and also at the installation of the Master of the Mercers' Company. Bernard Johnson's proposals for 'the reconstitution of the Court of Assistants, to provide both continuity and change in the membership' were approved and came into effect at the next Charter Day in 1947. The new Court comprised 18 members, as laid down in the Charter. This remains unchanged, and confirms the thoroughness of his review.

Above: Flood levels in the Undercroft.

Below right: HRH The Princess Royal takes tea with Governor Paul Crombie after being sworn in as an honorary member at the Cold Marts Court, 24 November 1949.

The great flood of March 1947 'invaded the Undercroft and Chapel to a record height of 3ft 4in above floor level'; this was to be repeated periodically until flood barriers were finally built several decades later. Considerable efforts were made to extend the membership, particularly those from the wool and cloth centres of the West Riding. During the year 30 new members joined the Company – a yearly increase of over 25 per cent. When Sheldon handed over to his successor in 1947, the Company had been re-energised, and a campaign begun for a university in York that would have far-reaching consequences for the city (*see box, p.80*).

An appeal to raise £12,000 for the restoration of the premises was launched at the Cold Marts Court in December 1947, when it was emphasised that the purpose was not just to preserve the ancient building, 'but to enable the Hall to be more fully used'. Oliver Sheldon called on the business houses of the city and the county, 'the descendants of the earlier merchants of York', to 'pay their tribute to the cradle from which their businesses came'. By the following April Charter Day £9,000 had been raised, including £2,000 from the Pilgrim Trust and a contribution from the London Mercers' Company.

Life progressed in 1948, with the newly reformed Court of Assistants meeting seven times during the year. Noel Terry presented a pair of 18th-century staves for the Wardens which are used today, while Governor Arthur Rymer attended a luncheon in

The Genesis of the University of York

It is difficult to imagine York today without its university. The fact that it exists at all is due in large part to the efforts of members of the Company. Of the many contributions that the Company and its predecessors have made to York since 1357, the creation of the University of York is arguably the greatest.

As far back as 1646, the Corporation (with the Company's support) sent a petition to Cromwell for the establishment of a university of York, with Bedern Hall as its nucleus. Periodic campaigns in later years were equally unsuccessful and by the 1940s it was felt that the opportunity to establish a university in the city had passed. However, the growing national awareness in post-war Britain of the urgent need to increase university education persuaded Oliver Sheldon that the time was ripe for one more effort. Two months into his year as Governor, through letters to *The Times* and relentless and skilful lobbying, Sheldon put the idea of a university in York on the national agenda. He asked the Archbishop of York, a fellow member, to preach the Thomas Herbert Sermon at the Michaelmas Court on 18 October 1946. In his sermon, entitled 'The Value of History', the Archbishop (very likely at Sheldon's request) spoke strongly in favour of the foundation of a university in York and Sheldon later published this sermon at his own expense.

Below: *Governor Oliver Sheldon, centre, with Archbishop Garbett, right, at the 1946 Michaelmas service at which the Archbishop preached on 'The Value of History'.*

Bottom: *The University of York today.*

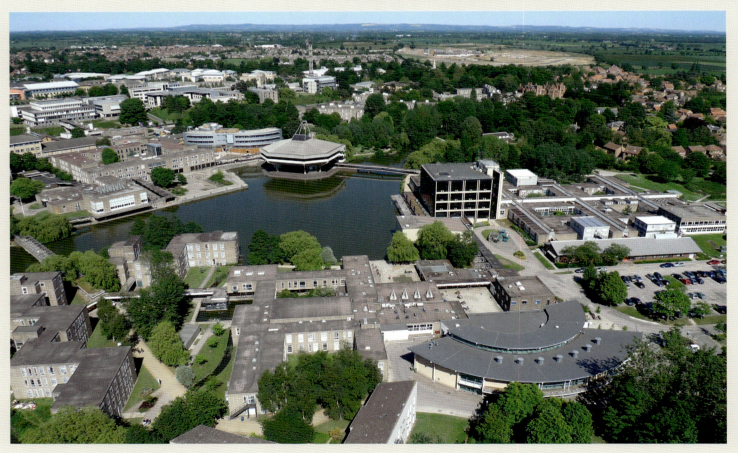

The early ideas (including the proposal that the King's Manor should be designated for future university use) were developed by the 'York University Foundation Council', an unofficial committee led by Sheldon as a very active secretary. This was later renamed the Academic Development Committee (ADC) which ran from 1949–56. It operated as a committee of the York Civic Trust which provided offices and significant administrative support. Sheldon continued to lead the campaign until his unexpected and greatly lamented death in August 1951 at the age of 57. The interest of the city waned, and in 1956 the ADC became the York Academic Trust (YAT) which operated independently. From its inception the YAT became the prime mover in the campaign for the establishment of the University. Its membership included individuals from the Merchant Adventurers, York Civic Trust and the city as a whole. JB Morrell and Arthur Rymer (whose business acumen was invaluable) played leading roles along with the Dean of York and Donald Barron as Treasurer.

The continuing efforts of the YAT bore fruit when they received a letter from the University Grants Committee saying that the application had been successful and York would have its University. In 1963 the new University of York received its charter, and the first students were admitted – 17 years after the Archbishop's Michaelmas sermon.

The University is an international success. In less than 50 years it has become one of the UK's top ten universities and one of the top 100 universities in the world. It is York's main employer and, together with tourism, is the prime economic driver of the city which has a developing technology-led economy that simply would not be possible without the University.

The establishment of the University against the odds had been a mighty team effort. Unquestionably Archbishop Garbett's Michaelmas sermon in the Hall had been the catalyst that sparked the initial civic effort. At various times the Company and certainly the York Civic Trust made significant contributions with the York Academic Trust acting over eight years finally bringing the project to fruition. The collective belief and resolve of those numerous organisations and individuals (many of whom were Company members) fostered the idea over 16 years and this had been absolutely critical in the grant of the Charter. However, without Sheldon's vision and determination to seize the moment in the summer of 1946 during his year as Governor, the campaign would never have gained the necessary momentum to persuade the authorities of the day to grant York its university.

Regrettably, the contribution of Oliver Sheldon and other members of the Company to the founding of the University of York rarely receives the recognition it deserves.

The King's Manor is now part of the University of York.

Left: *A dinner in the Hall c.1950 by Alfred Gill.*

Below: *The Governor's Jewel.*

London given by the Master Mercer. That company's hall had been completely destroyed by bombings in 1941, and the luncheon was held in the kitchen, the only room apart from the cellars that survived.

Thanks to the perseverance of members, the Company ended an exceptionally hard decade in a stronger position than it began. HRH the Princess Royal was sworn in as an honorary member in 1949 before the largest recorded number of members; this was televised by BBC Leeds and transmitted throughout Yorkshire. Her Royal Highness was the first member of the Company from the Royal Family, and she attended the Jane Stainton Service the following year. The newly built Muniment Room and Museum were now operational, and members and the public were able to view the Company treasures. The Yorkshire Law Society dined by candlelight on the first occasion that the Hall was used for a major dinner since before the War, and the Appeal Fund had reached a sufficient level to enable restoration of the Chapel to begin.

Below left: *The Hall in 1964, before the development of adjacent properties.*

Below: *The Venison Feast, November 1952. Governor Christopher Rowntree (left) with the Lord Mayor of York (centre) and visiting Masters.*

Above: *The English Cheese Council meets in the Hall in 1960.*

Below right: *HRH The Duchess of Kent receives honorary membership of the Company from Governor Lewis Waddilove at a Special Court on 30 September 1978.*

1950s and beyond

As life returned to normal, attention was given to matters other than the building. When Governor George Herbert attended the Mercers' Feast in London, he noted that he was the only master without a badge of office, and concluded that the Company should have one. The following year, Lancelot Foster presented the Governor's Jewel. Ceremonial robes were also purchased for £18 12s. 6d.

The Venison Feast was resurrected in January 1951 with 50 members attending. There had been great difficulty in sourcing the venison in January, but fortunately Lord Barnard saved the day by giving two hinds from his park at Raby Castle. As 'a noble celebration of the Company's 600th year', Past Governors subscribed £200 for the purchase of a letter from Elizabeth I in which she complained in outspoken terms of an imperial edict favouring the Hanseatic merchants and excluding the English merchants from trading in the empire, thus proving once again that many things alter but nothing changes. This letter is still in the Company archives.

Additional Fossgate shops were purchased in 1963. This was done not just to ensure future income, but also, as Governor Ian Crombie said, to 'maintain a barrier of period property between our Hall and the area of modern development'. The Hall was actively marketed for the first time in 1969, when it was widely advertised and show cards were sent to hotels, coach operators and travel agents throughout Yorkshire and neighbouring counties.

From 1970 onwards, increasing efforts were made to improve the Hall and make it more attractive to visitors and a source of pride for members. The magnificent Coat of Arms displayed above the dais in the Great Hall was carved by member Dick Reid and presented at the 1971 Venison Feast. The paintings were returned from the Art Gallery, the maces reconditioned and displayed in the Governor's Parlour, and the banners cleaned and re-hung. A Government indemnity enabled the Company silver to go on display for the benefit of the public. These improvements substantially increased the number of visitors.

The death of Noel Terry in 1980 was greatly regretted; he was a Past Governor and had been exceptionally generous to the Company. His obituary recorded that 'He hated publicity … he did good almost by stealth.'

Finances remained a concern and it was unanimously agreed that the voluntary contribution from members should be £2. 2s. 0d. per annum towards the running costs of the Company. However, the cost of maintaining the property increased relentlessly and overshadowed everything for the next four decades, with successive Governors highlighting the position amid calls for yet another appeal. In 1958 Governor Denys Creer noted that 'the few

reserves that we still have left are fast disappearing in meeting running expenses and will soon be entirely exhausted.' Nearly ten years later, in 1967, Governor Mark Horsley launched 'the third, and, it was hoped, the final appeal for the restoration of the Hall.' He later reported that 'the work has been done in a most admirable manner, and we can reasonably hope that no further major repairs in the Hall will be needed in the foreseeable future'.

Sadly, this optimism proved to be unfounded, and in 1978 Governor Lewis Waddilove was still concerned about the future administration of the Company's affairs and 'the need for some structure … which will relieve the Governor from a sense of living on the edge of crisis'. This was just as true in 1982 when Governor Michael Saville reported the need to spend 'considerable sums of money in coming years on the essential upkeep and improvement of The Hall … Careful and prudent planning will be essential in raising any necessary finance'.

The 1980s were an important time in the development of the Hall. A far-sighted group of members (Reg Stephenson, Michael Saville, John Rymer, Sir Peter Shepherd and Jack Birch) implemented an agreed programme as they succeeded each other as Governors. This produced a step-change in the development of the Hall as a source of revenue.

The Hall had always been a cold and, it has to be said, at times an unwelcoming place; as stated earlier, it required four days to produce a comfortable temperature. To remedy this, new central heating was installed in 1982. After a grant, the cost to the Company was £20,000, which was paid by Sir Peter Shepherd. The new controls were not immediately mastered and conditions for the Venison Feast were closer to the Sahara than the Arctic. During Grace, an older member was overcome by heat and was carried out only to return when the temperature had been reduced by opening every window and door. A training programme immediately followed.

The Clerk, David Stewart, greets HRH The Duchess of Kent as she arrives at the Hall to receive honorary membership.

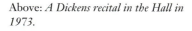

Above: *A Dickens recital in the Hall in 1973.*

Left: *Three far-sighted governors: Sir Peter Shepherd, John Rymer and Michael Saville.*

Above: *Senior Warden Peter Herbert with the Clerk, Ivison Wheatley, on their way to deliver gifts to the Company's pensioners in 1988.*

THE CLERK

Right: *Colonel James Finlay (left) hands over as Clerk to Captain Stephen Upright RN in July 2010.*

For many generations events at the Hall were organised by an honorary Clerk, but since 1985, when Ivison Wheatley was appointed, the position has been a salaried one. James Finlay, Clerk 1998–2010, noted that the Clerk acts as the 'chief executive' of the Company, and has a wide range of responsibilities. The Clerk today must be administrator, bookkeeper, landlord, minutes secretary, building manager, museum curator, tour guide, and organiser of events in the Hall, from small lunches to formal receptions and the annual Michaelmas and Venison feasts. In the few months following his appointment as Clerk in 2010, Stephen Upright arranged dinners, hosted a pantomime dame, staged a medieval mystery play, installed a credit-card terminal and conducted candlelit tours of the Hall. It is a varied and challenging role, as Ivison Wheatley recalls, almost like running a small stately home.

The Clerk is supported by a dedicated staff, by architects, legal, financial and curatorial advisers and other professionals, as well as by volunteer curators.

The new heating was pivotal and instantly transformed the Hall into a much more pleasant place to meet and dine. Lettings to external parties rocketed, leading to a significantly increased income from Hall hire which is still the largest single source of Company income. However, the growing activity levels of the Company were putting an increasing load on the Governor and David Stewart, the hard-working voluntary Clerk who was in his 80th year. Governor Waddilove had previously highlighted the need 'for some structure which will relieve the Clerk of a burden that is becoming intolerable'. Despite the financial difficulties, it was agreed that the Company urgently needed a salaried full-time Clerk and Ivison Wheatley was sworn in as Clerk at the 1985 Charter Day court. David Stewart retired after 19 years of exceptional service and was given a typewriter to replace the one he had used for many years on Company business! Constant preoccupation with maintaining the building did not prevent the Company from playing a role in the city and beyond,

and the newly appointed Clerk added a new impetus to both internal and external Company activities.

Although members were no longer driven by concerns about trade as their predecessors had been, a strong sense of enterprise still pervaded the Company. Discussions were held with the Company of Cutlers in Hallamshire, resulting in a series of enterprise lectures, the venue alternating between each Company's Hall. The first lecture, with many Cutlers attending, was given by Sir Monty Finniston in the Hall in December 1986. In later years, the Chairman of the Stock Exchange and the President of the Confederation of British Industry (CBI) also gave lectures in the Hall. Schools were encouraged to use the Hall and the 1988 Trust was established to widen charitable giving to 'the advancement of education generally in the UK and Northern Ireland … in the study of commercial and industrial organisations and activities'.

With an air of inevitability, the issue of Hall maintenance costs resurfaced in the late 1980s. In

LINKS WITH OTHER COMPANIES AND GUILDS

The Company enjoys links with many other companies and guilds in London, Bristol, Shrewsbury, Sheffield, Edinburgh and Glasgow, and closer to home in York and Richmond, North Yorkshire.

The seven guilds and companies of York work closely together on many matters of mutual interest and their Clerks meet formally on a quarterly basis. Slightly further afield, the Company enjoys close links with other Yorkshire guilds and companies, including the Company of Cutlers in Hallamshire, the Company of Mercers, Grocers and Haberdashers, and the Company of Fellmongers, both from Richmond, North Yorkshire. The Company is particularly proud of these Yorkshire connections and is privileged to be invited to attend events in Sheffield and in Richmond including the St George's Day and Corpus Christi celebrations.

Within the square mile of the City of London there are more than 100 guilds where they are known as livery companies, some very old and some recently formed to reflect modern life. We have links with 11 of them. The origins of livery companies are no different to any other guild or company formed to foster its own trade or craft. The London companies are listed in

The Lord Mayor of London, David Lewis, admires the Governor's Jewel worn by Governor Professor Anthony Robards at a dinner in London in 2008.

order of seniority. The senior 12 companies are known as 'The Great Twelve' and we have links with five: The Worshipful Companies of Mercers (1), Grocers (2), Drapers (3), Goldsmiths (5) and Haberdashers (8). The links are fostered by dinners and other social occasions. The Governor of the day receives a generous welcome in many splendid halls across the country, and that hospitality is returned with invitations to either the Michaelmas or Venison Feast in the Hall.

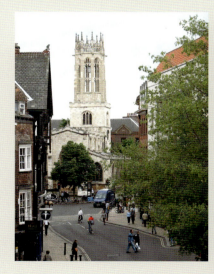

Above: *The Guild Church of All Saints Pavement.*

Right: *The Governor and Clerk at the Richmond Mercers' St George's Day celebrations in 2010.*

1987, Governor Sir Donald Barron warned that the Company would have to 'face up to the likelihood of heavy expenditure quite soon. No doubt we shall have to mount an Appeal.' He did add that the Hall was warmer and more welcoming now, and hence more popular, thanks in large part to the attention given to the heating system four or five years previously. An appeal was launched in 1992. Led by Sir Donald Barron and with a strong team, it had raised £400,000

within three years. This significant sum was a 'get out of jail card' as for the first time it put available resources ahead of the immediate property needs. This enabled a planned programme to be executed over time rather than yet another round of 'urgent repairs'.

Despite property concerns, activities continued to grow. Policy groups reviewed 'the composition and number of the membership', 'religious, social and charity matters' and 'business and enterprise'. The first business breakfast was held in 1992 and when the Hall was registered for civil weddings, it became one of the most sought-after venues in the city. In collaboration with York University a series of science discovery lectures was inaugurated in March 1997 and was attended by a capacity audience of members and the public. Professor Skerry talked on bone tissue, one of the important discoveries being made at the University. The first golf match with the York Merchant Taylors was held in 1998 resulting in a 'calculated draw'. This continues to be a keen contest and loss of the trophy during his year is a matter of anxiety for any Governor.

Links with the Armed Forces have always been very important, and representatives from all three Services are invited to the annual Venison Feast. Each year the Governor presents engraved tankards to regular, reserve and cadet members of the three Services at a ceremony attended by families and unit representatives. It is an evening much valued by members and guests alike. Since the mid-1980s the Company has enjoyed an affiliation with HMS *York*. When the ship is at a nearby port, hospitality is shared and a 'day at sea' is a highlight. By the turn of the century a formal link was established with the Prince of Wales's Own Regiment of Yorkshire, continued today by the Yorkshire Regiment.

Right: *The Hall packed to capacity for a lecture.*

Centre: *Professor David Smith of the Department of Chemistry at the University of York, gives the 14th annual Science Discovery lecture on 18 March 2010.*

Below left: *Governor Dick Reid on the bridge of HMS* York *in 1993.*

Below right: *Presentation of tankards to regular, reserve and cadet members of the Armed Services in 2011.*

Exchanges with RAF Linton-on-Ouse are regular, and fortunate is the Governor who has an opportunity to fly during his year.

To realise its full potential, one more heave would be required to bring the Hall to the highest standards of other visitor attractions. A grant from the Heritage Lottery Fund in 2002 financed essential improvements such as a lift and disabled access. This grant, together with £100,000 raised by a Company appeal led by Trevor Copley (Governor 2000–1), also covered the appointment of an audience development officer for three years and the development of an audio tour guide. This hard work was subsequently rewarded with regular tourism awards and the many congratulatory comments in the visitors' book confirm the success of the audio guide. To maintain this progress a full-time Hall Manager was appointed in 1997.

Eleven members (and spouses) paid a highly successful visit to Hamburg in 2002 to re-establish contact with a city which had played a leading part in the Company's fortunes for nearly 300 years. The 650th anniversary of the building of the Hall was marked by a 'Meet the Merchants Exhibition' in December 2006 and a reception on 10 May 2007, when the Company was graced by the presence of honorary member HRH The Duke of York. Later that year the Company organised an academic conference that attracted a number of leading scholars working on medieval merchants and guilds. It was appropriate that Dr Peter Addyman, an internationally acclaimed archaeologist (responsible for the discovery of the

major Viking settlement in York) was then Governor. A business leaders' event has been introduced and brings 100 of York's leaders together for an annual lecture and networking evening. When the Bank of England Monetary Policy Committee (MPC) held meetings in Yorkshire, the Hall was the natural venue for a lunch for the members of the MPC and City leaders.

New state-of-the-art LED lighting was installed and the heating updated in March 2009. This dramatically

improved the appearance, particularly the illumination of the splendid roof timbers: 'We can now see right up to the roof and it adds ten feet to the height of the building,' said a member. The long road to enhance the Hall culminated in the grant of unconditional accreditation by the Museums, Libraries and Archives Council in October 2009. This confirmed that the Hall and its collections met the highest national standards and as an accredited museum it would be eligible for grants and collaborative opportunities with other major institutions. This success is an appropriate tribute to all those who have striven to improve conditions at the Hall since 1945.

Modern technology easily repelled a return of the dreaded death-watch beetle in 2009. In earlier years, this would have led to panic and the fumigation of the building (not always appreciated by visitors and staff). Instead, a specialist company 'cooked' the beetles during their dormant stage by warming the infected pillars above 50°C. This allowed the Hall to remain open to the public and the process almost became a visitor attraction in its own right.

In March 2010 the Company organised and hosted a visit to Yorkshire by the German Ambassador, Herr Georg Boomgaarden, accompanied by his wife Christiane. Their visit included York, the Port of Hull, the east coast, the University of York, the National Rail Museum, and an audience with the Archbishop. The Ambassador and Governor co-hosted a dinner in the Hall for 180 influential people from all walks of life and every part of Yorkshire, during which David Hockney was observed sketching one of the speakers on his iPhone. An arts event has been added

to the Science Discovery Lecture. Both are open to the public, and on these occasions the Great Hall is always full to capacity.

Today

It is 72 years since the Court was discussing air-raid shelters and sandbags, and the Company is incomparably stronger than it was in 1939. As the last few pages have shown, it has not been an easy path, but

THE COMPANY PENSIONERS

The hospital founded in the Undercroft of the Hall by the Fraternity of Our Lord Jesus and the Blessed Virgin Mary in the 14th century provided for the support of 13 'poor or feeble persons', a figure thought to reflect Christ and the 12 Apostles.

The number of 'hospitallers' and the conditions in which they lived varied over the centuries. It is not known exactly when they were no longer expected to reside in the Undercroft, but as late as the 19th century there were bedrooms for men and women, although many of those receiving support appear to have lived out, coming to the Hall to collect their pensions.

By 1985, only one pensioner remained. It was decided then to revive the tradition of support for the elderly in the spirit of the original licence, and nine further pensioners were appointed. In 1996 the number was increased to the original 13. Today, the wardens visit the pensioners in their homes twice a year, at Christmas and in the summer, when small pensions are paid, and a tea party is held every summer under the guidance of the Deputy Governor.

*Below right:
Pensioners' tea party in the Undercroft.*

Below: The German Ambassador and his wife view the Company's archive.

thanks to the unfailing efforts of members during and since the War, the Hall today is in many ways in better condition than it has ever been. It is almost certainly the finest medieval building of its type in the world in daily use, and one of the main tourist attractions in the city.

The early members would envy the warm and stable conditions that modern technology provides. No more is it necessary, as in the past, to open a meeting in the Great Hall and immediately adjourn to the warmth (and light) of the Blue Bell, a few doors away. Now the Hall is always warm, even on the coldest of days. The new lighting system installed in 2009 gives much greater clarity to the structure, paintings and artefacts; lighting scenarios can be changed to enhance particular events. State-of-the-art monitoring systems maintain security and highlight problems early so that routine maintenance does not become a major and costly repair. The Foss flood barrier should mitigate future flood damage.

Thanks to prudent and sometimes courageous investment, the Fossgate properties are in excellent condition and fully let, with the rents generating 20 per cent of Company income. Members who pioneered the investment immediately after the War would be especially pleased with their work.

Looking to the future

The maintenance and improvement of the Hall has dominated the efforts and finances of the Company throughout its existence and will always be the prime duty of the membership. Future serious and unpredictable risks are inevitable, but there is reason to hope that for the first time for many centuries the costs of maintaining and improving the fabric will not sap the Company's energy and finances to such an extent as in the past. Freedom from building concerns will enable the Company to develop further its external activities.

The Company is very aware of this and has a will, and now the opportunity, to play a growing role in the city and region; the current membership is working hard and purposefully to realise this vision. This will be in a very different way from 650 years ago but the core values give a clear direction. It is likely to be more of a supporting and facilitating role, with particular emphasis on fostering entrepreneurship and raising the profile and esteem of industry and commerce within its area of influence. Oliver Sheldon (Governor 1946–7) summarised it well when he said: 'I believe our Company and our Hall will only fulfil their due place in our modern social life if they continue, as in the past, to be of use and service.'

THE COMPANY COAT OF ARMS

The Company was granted its coat of arms in 1969: Barry wavy argent and azure on a Chief per pale Gules and Azure a Lion Passant Or between two Roses Argent barbed and seeded proper. And for the Crest on a Wreath Argent and Gules Leaping from Water barry wavy Argent and Azure a Pegasus Argent winged Azure hooved Or. On either side a Pegasus Argent hooved Or the wings Azure each charged with a Rose Argent barbed and seeded proper.

The white roses represent Yorkshire, while the lion is the national emblem for England. Pegasus, the winged horse, and the waves, symbolise travel over water, illustrating the role of the Merchant Adventurers who traded overseas, and the French motto 'Dieu nous donne bonne aventure' means 'God prosper our venture'.

THE HALL TODAY

BEHIND THE SCENES AT A COMPANY EVENT

Social events have always been an extremely important part of the life of the Company and remain so today. One of the founding purposes of any medieval guild was fraternity and today this remains one of the Company's core purposes. A wide range of events is held each year including informal lunches, breakfasts, lectures, members' evenings and summer parties, as well as more formal dinners. The largest and most formal of these is the annual Venison Feast held on the Friday before the first Saturday in November. It is a full 'livery' dinner attended by many members and their personal guests as well as official guests of the Company. It is the role of the Clerk and the Company's staff to make the arrangements for all of these events.

The Governor acts as the host at the Venison Feast. The Clerk therefore must work extremely closely with him and his spouse to make the necessary arrangements. The first major task that falls to the Governor is to identify and invite his guest speaker. This will normally be done at least one year in advance. Then the official guest list must be confirmed. Official guests are invited so that hospitality may be reciprocated or thanks offered for a particular service. For reasons of cost and space the official guest list is strictly controlled by the Court of Assistants and may not be varied without its approval. A caterer is booked and the process of selecting the menu and wines starts. The Clerk confirms the bookings with the Master of Ceremonies, musicians, photographer and any other 'extras' the Governor might require. Arrangements for flowers and table decorations are made. Only then can an accurate budget be prepared and the ticket costs for members and their private guests set.

About four months before the event, letters of invitation are sent to official guests. Members are then invited to bid for places and one month before the dinner numbers are confirmed. Hotels are booked for guests and 'pour memoire' invitation cards are sent to everyone who is due to attend together with the necessary administrative details. At this stage the final detailed planning starts in earnest and the work level of the Hall staff becomes somewhat frenetic! Meetings are held with the caterer, menu cards prepared and sent to the printers and the seating plan is drafted and approved by the Governor before in turn being printed.

Far right: The tables are laid.

Below: Hall-Keeper Trevor King prepares the wine for a Company event.

And then the day of the event dawns: the caterer arrives, the Hall is arranged, the tables are laid, the lighting is adjusted and the silver put in place. The Hall looks magnificent. In the kitchens the chefs start to work their miracles by preparing a complex dinner for more than 180 guests in almost medieval conditions. At the due time guests arrive, are greeted warmly by the Governor and his officers and after a welcoming drink take their places for dinner which is served faultlessly by the immaculately dressed catering staff. Following the Loyal Toast, the speeches are made and are warmly applauded. Eventually everyone leaves having attended an evening of great friendship and conviviality that has, of course, gone without a hitch.

Well, that may be the theory but it is not always the case. Even if it is not, the Clerk and the Hall staff will do everything they can to ensure that those attending do not notice. Sometimes they succeed. Some problems are small and can be easily solved, but others may be more serious. When the Venison Feast was held on Friday 3 November 2000, York was seriously flooded. Following careful consideration, the Governor decided that it should go ahead and the

majority of guests battled the water and arrived on time. Halfway through dinner the Clerk was called to the telephone to be advised by the Environment Agency that should the water in the River Ouse rise by a further two inches the flood barrier would be over-topped and the Hall flooded.

This was not welcome news and, following a quick consultation with the Governor, the decision was made to remove the cheese course, cancel the Loving Cup ceremony and shorten the speeches. It was the first of these decisions that caused the biggest problem. One member, oblivious to the looming catastrophe outside, objected in the strongest possible terms to the loss of his cheese course and the Clerk was summoned to explain himself. The Clerk and the Hall staff then cleared the

Above left: *Executive Secretary Christine Hemingbrough and Senior Hall-Keeper Bruce Wray wait to greet guests at the 2010 Venison Feast.*

Above right: *Chef at work in the kitchen.*

Above: *The first course is laid out in the Great Hall.*

Undercroft of everything, including the silver display, with the Clerk managing to drop one piece on the floor much to the irritation of the Honorary Curator of Silver. In the event the flood defences held and the Feast was judged to be a great success. The following morning the sky was blue and the swans were enjoying a swim in the moat of York Castle for the first time for several hundred years.

On another occasion a gas leak developed about three hours before dinner was due to be served. Northern Gas Networks decided it was unsafe and cut the gas off and then departed wishing us a good evening. No cooking could be carried out – something of a problem with 180 guests arriving very shortly. This did cause the Clerk's stress level to rise, but the Senior Hall Keeper calmly picked up the telephone and somehow found a solution. The gas was switched back on with one hour to go. The chefs worked miracles, the dinner was perfect, the Clerk's stress level reduced almost back to normal and most importantly no one knew that there had even been a problem.

Pre-dinner drinks after a Charter Day Court.

THE COMPANY AND CHARITY

In the centuries before the National Health Service, social security and government assistance for a variety of projects, charity was in the hands of the Church and the wealthy. People who had made substantial sums of money were persuaded that it was their Christian duty to assist those who were less fortunate than themselves. The archives of the Company detail many cases where 'poor and feeble persons' were supported by the membership.

Nowadays the focus is inevitably different. Possibly the most significant charitable work that the members of the Company perform is the conservation (and restoration when necessary) of the Hall. The members have an obligation to hand on the Hall to succeeding generations in as good a condition as possible.

Social security and health provision having been taken over by the government, the present members of the Company, in their outward-facing charitable work, have focused their attention on fostering entrepreneurship, particularly amongst the young.

Enterprise awards have been given and there have been (and continue to be) frequent discussions as to ways in which young people can be encouraged to emulate the entrepreneurial spirit of early Merchant Adventurers.

This concentration on enterprise is just one example of the ways in which the members of the Company have moved with the times while maintaining the charitable spirit of their medieval predecessors.

The running of the Hall

The Company's ancient Hall, a scheduled ancient monument listed Grade 1, remains in constant use today as it has throughout most of its long life. It is used for three main purposes: by the Company for its own business and social events; as an accredited museum open to the public throughout the year; and as a venue for private hire. These three and often conflicting uses mean that the Hall Manager has an extremely busy and demanding role to meet the differing requirements of the various users. Being an accredited museum visited by well over 20,000 paying visitors each year means that the Company has to meet national standards of museum conservation and display of both the Hall and its collections.

The use of the Hall as a venue for private hire is nothing new and although virtually all events today go without a hitch, this was not always the case. As we have seen, the minutes of a court held in 1695

reported disapprovingly that 'some damage had been done to the Tables, Formes, Benches, Windows and other things by such as have had liberty to Feast therein.' Three years later Sheriff Radley had to make good damages to the Hall caused during his Feast. Clearly they enjoyed good parties in the 17th century! In the 19th century the Hall tended to be used for more sober purposes – a school, meetings and lectures, although the Company did occasionally have 'sumptuous' breakfasts. The Company paid a caretaker to clean the Hall.

Above left: *Encouraging future entrepreneurs.*

Above: *Hall Manager Lauren Marshall discussing wedding plans with potential clients.*

Below: *The Hall is a popular venue for weddings.*

Today hire for private events provides an important part of the Company's income stream. It is a very popular venue for civil partnerships, receptions, corporate dinners and functions, lectures and many other similar events. In between the Hall being used as a museum and as a private hire venue, the Company's own business and social events have to be fitted in. All of this requires the Hall Manager to be something of a magician as well as a diplomat to meet the often conflicting demands of its differing uses and to ensure that the highest of standards are maintained at all times. The Hall Manager is assisted not only by the Company's small but dedicated staff, but also by the panel of five approved catering firms that are allowed to work in the Hall.

For a building that is more than 650 years old and largely original to be able to withstand the pressures of such constant and varied use throughout its long life is a very great tribute to the medieval carpenters who started to build it in 1357. They would be amazed if they were able to see it today.

Above right:
Hall-Keeper George Smith moving chairs in the Undercroft.

Right: Dusting the paintings in the Great Hall.

MEMBERSHIP

The Company today has around 160 ordinary Members all of whom become members either by patrimony or by invitation. The modern term is 'by invitation' but this was previously known as 'by redemption' meaning quite simply on payment. The term 'by redemption' is still in use in many Livery and other companies. The present-day interpretation of 'membership by

This page:
The gardens are maintained for the enjoyment of the public as well as visitors to the Hall.

patrimony' is that the member was born when one parent was a member of the Company.

Members are drawn from a very wide variety of professions and backgrounds. In 1998, there were no women members. Nowadays they represent an increasing proportion of the membership. Potential members must show that they will support the aims and objectives of the Company with enthusiasm and energy, and must meet certain criteria for membership approved by the Court of Assistants. A potential member must be proposed by a member of the Company supported by two further members who will act as seconders. Proposals for membership by patrimony will be nominated by the parent. Seconders are not required, but the individual must meet all the other criteria in exactly the same way as any other ordinary member.

Nearly six centuries of continuity are represented in the list of Masters and Governors. A new board on the right records Governors from 2009 onwards.

Proposals for membership are first considered by the Nominations Committee. This committee will then recommend names who might be invited to take up membership to the Court of Assistants. Following approval by the Court, successful nominees will be invited to attend the next Charter Day Court held annually in April, when they will be admitted to membership by taking the 'Oathe of Brethren of the Company of Merchant Adventurers of the City of York'. This ancient oath was first recorded as being used in the Company in 1495.

COURTS AND COMMITTEES

One of the earliest references to the appointment of officers of the Company is dated 5 February 1406/7 when King Henry IV granted to the English Merchants in the Low Countries 'The right to band together, elect their own Governors [in the plural] for the conduct of their affairs and to rectify their own abuses'. In the Royal Charter of 12 July 1430 the York Mercers and Merchants on the one hand patterned themselves on the Company of Merchant Adventurers of England by having a Governor, and on the other on the Merchants of the Staple of England by having two Constables. Their authority was however dependent on 'legislation agreed by the whole community or the majority thereof, or given by the Crown'. The Constables were later known as Wardens.

The Royal Charter of 1581 granted by Queen Elizabeth I perpetuated that authority be vested in the Company as a whole. That is to say the Governor, Assistants and Company are three separate parts of a triune body and the Governor has no authority unless it is delegated to him by the Company as a whole. The Governor alone or the Governor and Assistants together cannot enter into any legislative act without the consent of the whole Company. 'The Company' in this respect refers to the rest of the members apart from the Governor and Court of Assistants. This required the Company to meet formally on several occasions during the year. The two principal Courts were the Michaelmas Court and the Charter Day or 'Head' Court held on Lady Day, 25 March. Other special Courts were called as necessary; examples included the Synxon (Feast of St John) and Cold Mart (Cold Market) Courts. These Courts were based on important medieval cloth markets held in Antwerp each year to mark the four seasons. Today the Company meets formally once a year at the Charter Day Court.

The Charter provides for a Court of 18 Assistants to be presided over by a Governor who is not himself a member of the Court. Over the years the make-up of the 18 Assistants has evolved and today consists of the four officers (Immediate Past Governor, Deputy Governor and the two Wardens), five elected Past Governors and nine elected members. The Assistants are elected for a period of one year. The Company remains a Company incorporated by Royal Charter of 1581 from Queen Elizabeth I and has the Company registration number RC000137.

Oath taken by new members.

The Oath of the Bretheren of the Company of Merchant Adventurers of the City of York

Ye sweare to be trewe and faithfull to our Soveraigne Lady The Queen, her Heires, and Successors, and you shalbe obedyent to the Governor, his deputye, and assistants of the fellowshipp of Merchants; you shall come to all courtes and assemblies upon dewe warninge, havinge no reasonable excuse to the contrarye. You shall not willinglye do, consent, nor knowe to be done anythinge, that maye tend to the breache, violacon, or impeachment of anie the rights of this Companye. And if you knowe of anie thinge to be attempted or done to the contrarie, you shall, with all convenyent spede, discover, and shewe the same to the Governor or deputie for the time beinge. The counsell and previties of this saide commonaltye ye shall well and trewlie kepe. And all actes, ordinaunces, and institutions made and hereafter to be made, and standinge in force concerninge the good government and order of this fellowship, you shall on your parte maintene, supporte, and fulfill to your power and knowledge. So helpe you God.

In the time of *Richard Edward Haynes* Governor

Memorandum that *Colonel James Gideon Finlay OBE*

was admitted to the Freedom of the Company by Invitation on the Thirtieth day of September in the year of our Lord Two Thousand and Ten and took this oath

Clerk
Stephen Upright

Governor
Richard Haynes

New members are sworn in at the Charter Day Court in April 2010.

The Charter Day Court is in effect the Annual General Meeting and all members of the Company are entitled to attend. Traditionally held on Lady Day, it has more recently been delayed until mid-April for the practical reason of allowing a little more time for the preparation and audit of the Company's annual accounts. At the Court, the outgoing Governor presents a formal report of his year of office and the new Governor, officers, Assistants and honorary officials are elected thus giving the new Governor his authority for his year. The accounts for the previous year are formally adopted and new members recommended by the Court of Assistants are admitted. It is a formal affair and the officers wear their robes and badges of office.

Honorary officials include the Chamberlain who monitors the finances, the Chaplain, Architect and Legal Advisor. Honorary Curators for furniture and treen, paintings and ceramics, silver and jewellery, an Archivist, who has a salaried assistant, and a Curatorial Adviser, who is a senior and experienced museum professional, complete a strong and appropriately qualified team. Company business could not be conducted without the invaluable and committed contribution from all these individuals.

The Court of Assistants is the 'main board' of the Company, and the Governor and Assistants act as Trustees of the 1944 and 1988 Trusts on behalf of the Company. The Court meets formally four times a year. In addition to the Governor and 18 Assistants all Past Governors are entitled to attend and to express opinions on matters under discussion, but they are not entitled to cast a vote. The Court may, and does, co-opt others to attend meetings and the Honorary Chamberlain is one who is always present. The Court is served by the Clerk. The Court of Assistants has several sub-committees charged with various areas of the Company's business.

The very hard-working and dedicated team of a full-time Clerk, Hall Manager, Secretary and three Hall Keepers ensure that the Hall is maintained and always ready for the 200 events and 20,000 visitors it welcomes each year.

The Merchant Adventurers' Hall

The Merchant Adventurers' Hall

When, in December 1356, John Freboys, John Crome and Robert Smeton surveyed 'all that piece of ground with the buildings … now in Fossgate' newly acquired from Sir William Percy, they may have done so with some apprehension. As they walked down Fossgate towards Foss Bridge, the air would have been filled with the sounds and smells of the market in Pavement and the fish trades centred around the bridge itself. Turning aside, down a small passageway, they would have entered the Fossgate site. In front of them would have been a substantial but timeworn townhouse, surrounded by smaller buildings, its once-bright limestone walls now darkened by pollution from the many domestic and industrial hearths, and by the repeated flooding of the site by the nearby river Foss, to the south. Yet John Freboys and his fraternal brethren were men with a clear vision of how the site could be transformed. Around them, the city's streets were filled by the sound of building work. New timber-framed houses were rising, to two and sometimes three storeys above York's prosperous trading streets. We might imagine that on this winter's afternoon John Freboys and his fraternal brethren were accompanied by a master carpenter and mason, giving careful advice about how best this ancient townhouse could be transformed into a meeting hall for one of the city's most successful fraternities. Ahead lay ten years of building works, but perhaps even they would have been astonished that the building they constructed would still be standing some 650 years later.

The context of the building

Today, most visitors to the Merchant Adventurers' Hall approach it from the south-west via the 19th-century street of Piccadilly, but originally the main entrance to the Hall was from the north-east, via Fossgate. This was one of the city's most prosperous streets and home to many merchants, mercers and drapers. The street lay in the parish of St Crux, whose church provided the devotional focus and probably the earliest meeting place for the fraternity of Our Lord Jesus Christ and the Blessed Virgin Mary. The parish was also the home of crafts like the butchers, based in the nearby flesh shambles, and the saltwater fish trades, based around Fossbridge. The bridge was rebuilt in the 15th century, and the chantries

Previous pages: Interior of the north-east range.

Opposite: The north-east range and the Hall from the gatehouse.

Below: Fossgate from Foss Bridge.

of wealthy late medieval mercantile families such as the Blackburns were established in its Chapel of St Anne. Many of Fossgate's timber-framed houses were also being rebuilt and extended in the 14th and 15th centuries. Their burgage plots extended back towards the site of the fraternity hall.

To the south-west, the site of the Hall was bounded by a cobbled and cambered lane discovered in archaeological excavations in 1996. The lease of 1356 notes that Sir William Percy had only recently acquired the land from Robert Lisle and Thomas Duffield, co-executors of the deceased merchant, Henry Belton. There must have been some form of fences or boundaries further to the south-west, where Belton's land abutted that of one Henry Haxiholme. However, beyond this was an open area stretching towards the church of St Mary's, Castlegate, and to the Castle on Baile Hill and the city's Franciscan Friary. The Percys held the advowson (the right to nominate to an ecclesiastical living) of St Mary's and may have

acquired Belton's lands to facilitate the fraternity's ambitious building scheme. To the north-west was another small lane called 'Trichourlane' (probably on or near the present 'Tricksters lane'). To the south, the site was bounded by the river Foss, which regularly flooded as a result of the damming of the river upstream to create the castle moat and the King's fishpool.

The construction of the Hall

The problem of flooding was first addressed in the construction of the fraternity's guildhall. Archaeological excavations carried out by York Archaeological Trust in 1996 revealed that the previous house on the site, referred to as a 'mansum' in the deeds, was not demolished completely in 1356. Rather, it was ingeniously re-used as the foundations for the new building. A trench dug below the third window from the north-west revealed the remains of the building in the form of nine courses of fine-quality 'ashlar' masonry, which still retained traces

The Hall to the left, with the Minster in the distance.

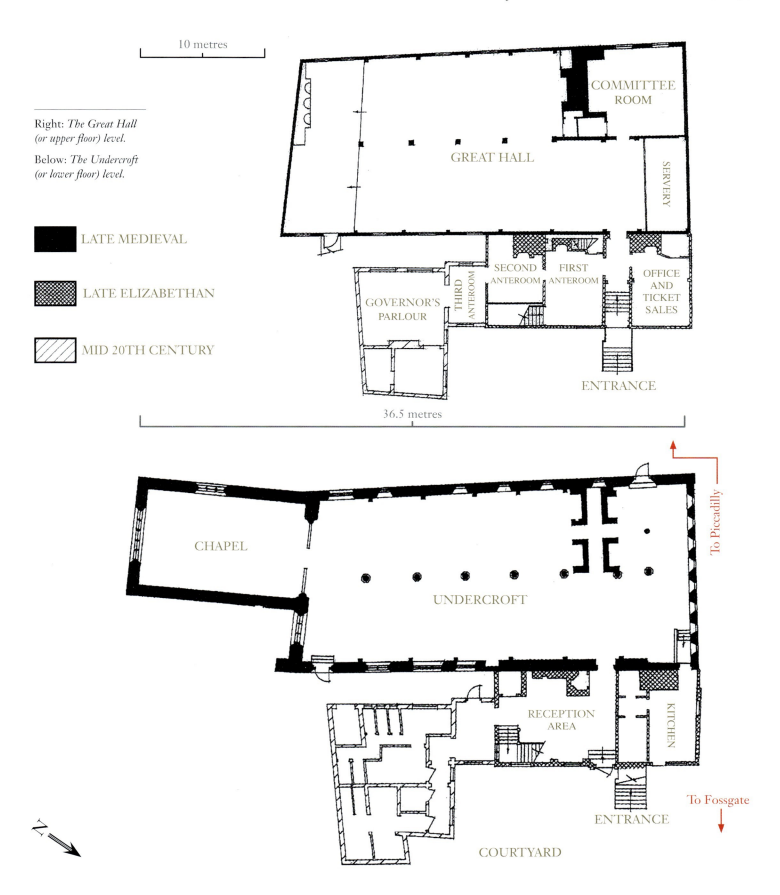

10 metres

Right: *The Great Hall (or upper floor) level.*

Below: *The Undercroft (or lower floor) level.*

LATE MEDIEVAL

LATE ELIZABETHAN

MID 20TH CENTURY

COMMITTEE ROOM

GREAT HALL

SERVERY

SECOND ANTEROOM

FIRST ANTEROOM

THIRD ANTEROOM

GOVERNOR'S PARLOUR

OFFICE AND TICKET SALES

ENTRANCE

36.5 metres

To Piccadilly

CHAPEL

UNDERCROFT

RECEPTION AREA

KITCHEN

ENTRANCE

To Fossgate

COURTYARD

N

3D images from the Company's website show the evolution of the Hall. The north-east range was added to the original medieval hall in the late 16th or early 17th century, and a new range was constructed in 1947.

of tooling and masons' marks dating to the late 11th or 12th century. The excavations also revealed a 'tide mark' on the Norman masonry, evidence of an episode of severe flooding of the site at some point in the 12th or 13th centuries. By building their Great Hall on top of the remains of the earlier townhouse, the fraternity of Our Lord Jesus Christ and the Blessed Virgin Mary hoped to avoid future floods. The 1996 excavations also showed that the ground level around the Great Hall had been raised by approximately 1.8m.

Above ground, the Merchant Adventurers' Hall still preserves much of the character and form of the late 14th-century building. In addition, the Company's archives contain a unique series of five account rolls dating to 1356–67, and an account book of 1358–69. The accounts shed valuable light on the purchase of building materials, on the labour force and craftsmen required to build the Great Hall, and on buildings which no longer survive on the site today. The rapid progress of building work suggests that the fraternity not only had the requisite funds to commence construction, but also a very clear vision of what they wanted in a guildhall.

What buildings or models might the fraternity have had in mind as a model for their new Great Hall?

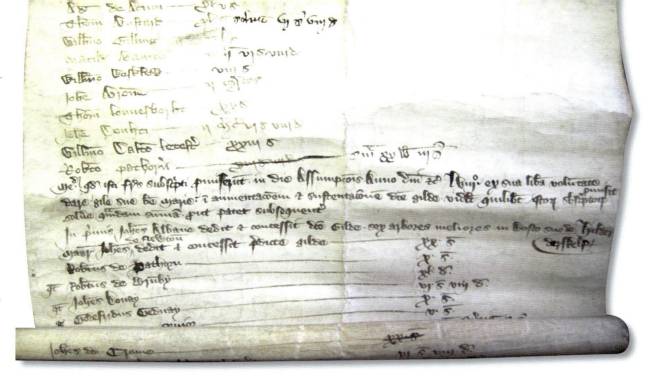

There were certainly other 'public' buildings in the city, such as the old Guildhall, located somewhere in the vicinity of the present Guildhall, and the Council chamber, on Ouse bridge, which probably dated to the 12th or 13th century. There were also numerous monastic buildings, churches and inns, in which many of York's guilds regularly met. However, Trinity Hall, as it became known, was more likely to have been inspired by the halls of the London guilds and fraternities, with which many of York's merchants may have been familiar, or by other provincial guildhalls, such as Boston (Lincolnshire), also being built at the same date. Importantly, many of these buildings were constructed on the site of, or were converted from, existing domestic buildings. Whatever the model for Trinity Hall, the building itself was to set the standard for a series of impressive guildhalls built in the following century. These included St John the Baptist's Hall in Aldwark (now the Merchant Taylors' Hall), St Anthony's Hall in Peaseholme Green (now the Quilters' Museum), the rebuilding of the Guildhall by the corporation and the St Christopher guild, and the now-lost halls of the Butchers in the Shambles and the Cordwainers in Hungate.

As was often the case with the London guildhalls, Trinity Hall was set back from the street frontage. It was accessed through a gatehouse and small courtyard, described in the 15th century as the 'halle warde'. The gatehouse was probably on the site of the modern Fossgate gatehouse, which was restored

in the 20th century, but which still preserves 15th-century fabric internally. It was probably always a two-storey structure, incorporating the surviving passageway and leading to an open space or 'ward' in front of the guildhall. It may well have had brightly painted and gilded images or statues of the Virgin or the Trinity on its façade, to signal the location of the Great Hall from the street. A second passageway from Fossgate into the site is also preserved slightly further to the east. Originally, this probably provided access directly to the Undercroft or to other buildings within the guildhall complex. A squint still preserved in the north-east wall of the Hall suggests that a close eye was probably kept on the comings and goings in the Great Hall ward.

Top: *Trefoil-headed window with fragments of its original stone dressings.*

Above: *The squint which once provided a view of comings and goings in the Hall ward.*

Above right: *The Hall was built of a mixture of new and re-used building materials.*

Right: *Tudor panelling in the Great Hall.*

The largest building on the Fossgate site was of course the Hall itself. Today, the early modern 'north-east range' obscures the original façade of the 14th-century building. However, it is possible to get an idea of the original appearance of the Hall from the south-west elevation towards Piccadilly. From here it is possible to see that the original ground floor of the building would have had a few courses of stone foundations below several courses of thin, dark-red medieval bricks. The account roll of 1366/7 records the carriage of nearly 3,000 of these 'tegulis muralibus' or 'wall-tiles' to the site, as well as the transporting of stone. The surviving accounts reveal the purchase and donation of other building materials for the 'Great Hall in a garden'. Timber for the massive Samson posts in the Undercroft, principal posts, and trusses of the Great Hall, window frames and wall panels came from a variety of woodlands as far afield as Bolton Percy, Acaster, Thorp Underwood, Wighill and Henderskelfe (now the site of Castle Howard). In total, over 530 trees were purchased between 1357 and 1361. Other timber was used in the construction of internal partitions and walls. There were cartloads of lime and plaster for rendering walls and partitions. Roofs were tiled and doors and windows furnished with ironwork. Many of the building materials may have been transported by river and offloaded at the guild's quay beyond Foss bridge. Some of them were recycled from buildings being demolished in nearby Pavement, and spare materials, particularly stone, was sold off and the profits returned to the building fund. As well as work on the Hall, the accounts refer to the construction and repair of other buildings around the site, such as fences and latrines.

Below: Over 240 individual computer-controlled LED lamps illuminate the 14th-century roof of the Great Hall.

Below right: The Undercroft.

The appearance of the medieval guildhall

From the surviving evidence within the building and from the documentary records, it is possible to reconstruct the original appearance of the building. The stone and brick of the ground floor of the building was probably plastered to give a unified appearance. Within this were a series of trefoil-headed windows with stone surrounds, fragments of which survive today. These may have been set further down the elevation, or they may originally have been much longer, narrow windows. The further raising of the ground levels around the building over time resulted in their being shortened to their present appearance. Fragments of the earlier building on the site were also

retained in the guildhall's 14th-century Undercroft, including the pointed arches of former windows still preserved towards the southern end of the elevation. At first-floor level the timber frame was probably left visible, but the brick infill panels between the timbers would always have been plastered. The form of the ground- and first-floor elevations also showed how space was divided internally into a series of 'bays', between pairs of principal posts.

In the centre of each bay was a medieval window. At first-floor level these would have taken the form of those still preserved at the north-western end of the building. The window frame was created by pegging intermediate studs into the wall plate at the top and the mid-rail below, and by a series of diagonally set mullions in between. It is unlikely that these were all glazed originally, since the surviving examples preserve grooves for oak shutters. The position of the windows in the centre of each of the bays of the Great Hall can be reconstructed from empty peg holes and, in the case of the third bay from the north-west, by the survival of the window frame in a bay into which a large back-to-back chimney was subsequently inserted. The windows at the southern end of both the south-west and north-east elevations seem to have been larger than elsewhere in the building. Here the wall plates preserve a series of empty peg holes, suggesting the presence of large, possibly projecting windows lighting this end of the Great Hall.

A close examination of the timber frame reveals that the small, intermediate 'close studs' in each bay are insertions, since they are cut rather than pegged into the rest of the frame. Originally the posts were simply ornamented by downward braces in an arrangement preserved in the interior north-east wall of the Hall as well as the exterior north-west elevation. Although the south-west and north-east elevations were therefore broadly similar, the Fossgate entrance must also have incorporated a two-storeyed porch, through which access could be gained to the first-floor hall. Although all traces of this structure were removed during the construction of the present north-east range, it contains several pieces of re-used timber which may have come from the original porch building.

Finally, it is worth considering the appearance of the gable ends of the 14th-century Hall. The north-western elevation has been preserved remarkably well,

and incorporates two surviving medieval windows, discovered and restored in the 20th century. The gable ends of the building were 'jettied' out over the ground floor in an impressive display of carpentry. But the north-western elevation also preserves a series of empty mortices in the underside of its jetty. These mortices are evidence that in contrast to the other walls of the Undercroft, the ground floor of this area of the building was originally timber-framed. The mortice would have received braces from a series of posts which survive internally. Looking more closely at the timber framing in the south-west elevation it is also possible to see that the northern end of the building has been extensively restored and replaced. So why was this area of the building constructed differently? And why has it evidently experienced problems such as subsidence

A pointed arch reveals the outline of the original window.

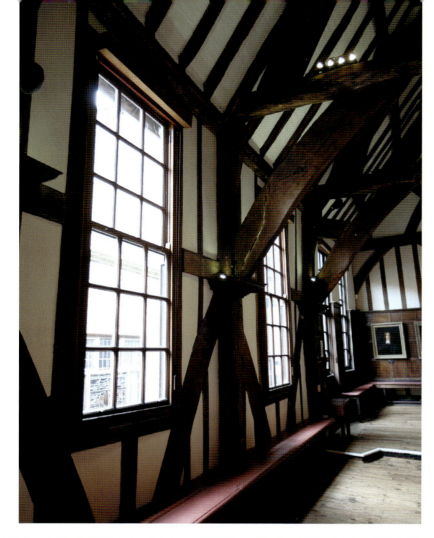

Top: *The sash windows in the Great Hall were installed in the 18th century.*

Above: *Traces of a medieval window in the Great Hall.*

more severely than other parts of the complex? It is possible that this part of the Hall does not share the same substantial 12th-century foundations as the remainder of the building. If so, it may have settled differently over time, and may also have been more vulnerable to damp and decay. Further excavations would be needed to explore this idea.

It is likely that originally the southern end of the Hall was very similar to the northern end, although it may have incorporated windows looking out over the river, evidence for which has now been lost due to the restoration of the gable ends, and the heightening of the Chapel roof in the late 16th century. The Chapel is a single-storey limestone building which abuts, and therefore post-dates the construction of the Great Hall. Although the stone is carefully coursed on the north-east and south-west elevations, the south-west side is a mixture of re-cut and re-used material, intermixed with tile and brick. The roof and the upper parts of the Chapel walls have been heightened, probably in 1667, when new fittings and fixtures in the interior resulted in the repositioning of windows. Scars and 'straight' joints in the walls and surrounding the windows indicate the original appearance of the Chapel. The present east window is a 19th-century replacement. The original stonework is preserved in the garden. It was originally slightly wider, and probably contained seven lights. There were two windows in the south-west elevation, one of which was removed entirely and the other re-set in the centre of the wall. There was also another window in the north-east elevation.

The date of the Chapel has long been debated by those working on Trinity Hall. In the 1940s, piecemeal excavations around the base of the chancel arch in the interior of the Undercroft revealed evidence of substantial foundations underneath the present building. This might suggest that the Chapel was also constructed on the site of an earlier building. Although the early records of the fraternity suggest that they maintained a close link with the parish church of St Crux, they also suggest that chaplains were celebrating mass in a small Chapel associated with the hospital. By 1411, however, this Chapel is described as 'by passage of years degenerated in grevious ruins'. It seems unlikely that this building could have been contemporary with the recently completed guildhall, unless it had been built by some very unscrupulous masons. However, it might well have been one of the buildings which survived from the 12th-century complex, re-used as a Chapel until sufficient funds had been raised for the new building in 1411. Indeed, the stone from the earlier Chapel may well have been re-used in the foundations and walling of the new building. An alternative location for the earlier Chapel is to the north-east of the Undercroft. Here, the walls are composed entirely of stone and preserve the remains of two earlier doorways, which appear to have connected the hospital to other structures. Whatever these buildings were, they appear to have been demolished or removed in the 15th century, when the walls were cut back and the present 15th-century windows inserted into this elevation.

The interior of the medieval guildhall:
The Undercroft, hospital and Chapel

Although the interior of the Merchant Adventurers' Hall has also been the subject of extensive repairs and restoration, it too provides important evidence of the original appearance of the building in the late 14th and 15th centuries. The most difficult space to reconstruct is perhaps the Undercroft, which accommodated the hospital for which a licence was granted in 1373. This area of the building is divided into two aisles and eight bays by a series of seven massive Samson posts. In the north-east wall the timber posts are supported by a series of six corbels, but this is only the case with the first post from the south-east in the south-western wall, whilst the others originally extended to ground level. However, all the posts within the Undercroft have been truncated because, despite the guild's best efforts to address the problems of the flooding of the site by the river Foss, this was a regular occurrence throughout its history and, indeed, within living memory. This resulted in the rotting and truncation of most of the posts and in the raising of the floor to its present level in the early 20th century. A sense of the original depth of the floor can be gained by looking through the glass panels along the south-west wall to where the posts have been mended using re-used ecclesiastical capitals and new timber scarfed onto the original wall posts.

Originally, then, the Undercroft was a much more impressive and lofty space, incorporating fabric in both the south-west and north-east walls from earlier buildings on the site. If the windows in the south-west wall were originally longer, they would have provided

Morning sun slants through the east window of the chapel.

more light, and indeed better ventilation, of the space. The walls would have been plastered and whitewashed with lime, into which small niches were set for candles, probably adjacent to the inmates' beds. Candles were also mounted onto iron prickets pressed into the surface of the Samson posts, which are covered in scorch marks. Underfoot, the floor was probably tiled simply with brick and compacted earth, overlain with rushes. Traces of these early floor surfaces were excavated by York Archaeological Trust in 1996.

Although it seems likely that originally the hospital was a relatively open space, lined with simple pallets, by the mid-15th century more substantial beds were constructed. The records refer to walling and plastering

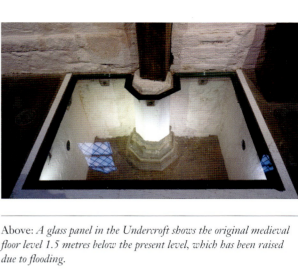

Above: *A glass panel in the Undercroft shows the original medieval floor level 1.5 metres below the present level, which has been raised due to flooding.*

associated with their construction, as well as the provision of curtains which could be drawn around them. The small, narrow brick walls or partitions excavated at the southern end of the north-east aisle in 1996 may well have been the remains of these structures.

It seems likely that the main entrance into the hospital was the impressive arched doorway through which visitors still pass today. Traces of soot-blackening at the northern end of the Undercroft suggest that these bays may always have been partitioned in some way from the remainder of the hospital. They may have provided accommodation for the Master or for the sisters of the hospital, responsible for the care of its inmates. The impressive four-fireplace structure

located at this end of the building is a later insertion. Originally, the hospital was probably only heated by portable braziers. The curtains provided for the beds were probably an important means of increasing the comfort, as well as the privacy, of their inmates.

By the 15th century, the most impressive space within the Undercroft was the Chapel. The archaeological evidence of windows preserved in the walls of the present building can be linked to documentary records of donations to the guild. They record that in 1490 William Cleveland, Master of the hospital, made general repairs to the masonry and bars of the Chapel windows, and spent £3. 13s. 4d. on a great glass window of seven panes at the high altar. In the same year alderman John Gilliot also paid for the making and repair of 'diverse' windows in the Chapel. Three years later the same men were involved in a further re-glazing scheme. William Cleveland, Thomas Fynch and the wife of the late John Ince 'made a glasse wyndow nexte unto the alter of the soweth sied of thare owne costis' and further down the south-west wall, the executor of Master Carre 'maide a glasse wyndow next of the same'. On the opposite side of the Chapel John Gilliot 'paid for glassyng the wyndow of the north seid, next unto the hye altar', and the contents of his window were later described as 'two ymages of Saint John and Saint Thomas' located over 'the altar of Saint Kateryn'. Although many parish churches had multiple altars and stained glass windows, Trinity Chapel was an unusually splendid example of how successive hospital Masters such as Gilliot and Cleveland sought to out-do each other in acts of patronage.

THE HOSPITAL

A medieval hospital was a religious institution that offered succour to the poor and unfortunate, but its primary purpose was a chantry, employing priests to say prayers for the souls of its founder and benefactors. Although it did not provide medical care in the sense that we think of a hospital today, it is likely that many of the inmates were infirm or bedridden and that the Chapel was deliberately positioned next to the Undercroft to enable the inmates to observe the celebration of mass from their beds if necessary.

The hospital in the Undercroft of the Hall was founded in 1371. On admission, inmates were provided with a bed, and with 'almus and all other esement'. Conditions for the first inmates were rudimentary. They probably slept on pallets of straw with sheets and coverlets, with men on one side of the Undercroft and women on the other. The nearest latrines were on the Foss, and were also used by other tenants in Fossgate. More substantial beds were provided for the men in 1437, while the women had to wait until the following year. The reference to plastering and walling in connection with the beds, and to the 30s. 4d. spent on 'curtens to beddys', suggests that the inmates were given more privacy at this stage.

Although it remained under the secular supervision of first the fraternity and then the Mercers' Guild, the hospital was in the charge of a master, supported eventually by other chaplains, and by lay staff to assist with the day-to-day care of inmates, which presumably involved cooking, cleaning and basic nursing if required. The Master's position was a powerful one. Being able to offer a bed to a poor person was regarded as a privilege, and there was sometimes friction between the Master and the merchants who oversaw the administration of the hospital. Efforts were made to preserve the Undercroft as a space where only the truly needy were accommodated.

The dissolution of the chantries in 1547 should have spelt the end of the hospital, but the Mercers' Guild argued that it was primarily a craft and charitable association, conveniently glossing over the religious sentiments that had dedicated so much property to the hospital. The merchants continued to administer the hospital and to support the inmates

with the income from property rents, bequests, gifts and members' fines which were known as brogues.

It is not clear exactly how the hospital operated in the 17th century. Not all of those admitted to the hospital lived in the Hall. In 1686, for instance, the widow Elizabeth Spence was given 'a place in our hospital with the usuall allowance' while at the same time Ellen Wainman was admitted to 'a Bedroome in our hospital (& noe more) and that upon hir good behaviour', suggesting that the allowance was more sought after than the room. Evidently Ellen behaved

A 15th-century woodcut by Jean Petit depicting a medieval hospital.

The hospital seal, showing the Coronation of the Virgin, depicted in stained glass in the chapel.

herself, for she was admitted with the usual allowance to a place in the hospital later that year. It is not hard to understand why the bedrooms would be a less appealing option than a cash allowance. The rooms must have been dark and damp, and the Undercroft was still liable to flooding. The wardens were ordered to pay the poor women in the hospital 3*s.* each in 1681, 'their goods & fuell having bin much damaged by the late high water.' Still, in the days before social security the hospital offered much-needed support for women in poverty, and there was no shortage of applicants petitioning for places as they became vacant. The unsuccessful were usually given some money from the poor box.

There were disturbing reports of intimidation in the 18th-century hospital. Complaints were made in 1722 that the hospital women and the Clerk 'exacted treats' from new inmates, and it was ordered that 'no treats nor money should be demanded for the future.' After further reports of 'divers abuses committed in the hospital by the ill behaviour' of the poor women in the hospital in 1735, the court proposed a 'scheme for better regulation' and recommended that an infirmary be provided 'in case of sickness'.

The exact process of appointment to a place in the hospital in the medieval and early modern period is unknown, but certainly by the 18th century applicants were interviewed in person and the successful candidate chosen by vote. Elizabeth Inman, a member's widow, was awarded her place in 1754 'by holding up hands', while Mrs Taylor,

also a widow of a member, 'having the greatest number of scrawls' was admitted in 1853. By the mid-19th century, there were men as well as women 'hospitallers', as they were known at the time, although it is still uncertain how many of them lived in the Undercroft. The Charity Commissioners' report of 1825 seems clear: 'The building consists of two large rooms under the company's hall in Fossgate, one of them being divided into sitting and sleeping rooms for five poor men, and the other in like manner for five poor women.' A plan of the Undercroft dated 1814 shows the separate bedrooms and apartments for men and women, but the two large rooms appear to have been let out, while the inmates' quarters are squeezed into a space that looks much too small to accommodate ten people. A minute of September 1858 notes that the painting and other repairs of the Hall and almshouses had been completed, and that 'all the Hospitallers but one were residing on the premises', which might suggest that there were other apartments or almshouses other than in the Undercroft itself.

As late as September 1893 the hospital was still occupied – the service in the chapel that year was cancelled 'owing to serious illness in one of the Rooms connected with the Merchants' Hall' – but the precise date when it was closed to inmates has yet to be identified. The Undercroft was restored in the 1920s, and by then the hospital, more than 500 years old, had closed, although support for the elderly continues to be an important part of the Company's activities (*see box, p89*).

The Great Hall

Although the Merchant Adventurers' Great Hall, located at first-floor level, has been subject to extensive programmes of repair and restoration in the 19th and 20th centuries, it too preserves remarkable evidence for its early appearance. Originally, the Great Hall would have been entered at first-floor level, through the present main entrance via a porch from the Hall ward. The squint, which once provided a view of the comings and goings in the courtyard, still survives, but was blocked by the construction of the north-east range in the 16th and 17th centuries. However, it is possible to imagine how it would have been used to keep a lookout for prominent guests arriving at the Great Hall, so that a cue could be given to the musicians in the gallery which was once located above the 'screens passage' entrance into the Great Hall. Although no traces of this structure survive today, there are records of its removal in the 20th century, and scorch marks in the horizontal tie beam above the entrance bay indicate the presence of candles and lights here, in the past.

The Great Hall.

The Great Hall, like the Undercroft, is a double-aisled, eight-bay structure. It is divided into what is sometimes referred to as a 'tripartite' arrangement, consisting of a 'low' end, containing a buttery and pantry for storage, separated by the screens passage from the remainder of the Great Hall. The partition wall which now separates the Committee Room from the Great Hall is a later insertion, as is the impressive back-to-back fireplace located here. The Great Hall did have some form of heating provision, however, since strings for a louvre to facilitate the dispersal of smoke are recorded in the early account rolls. At the southern end of the Great Hall was the 'high' dais end, where the master and the wardens of the guild would sit during the fraternity feasts and business meetings. This area was probably always raised slightly above the rest of the floor, although sadly the original floorboards have long since been replaced. The importance of this area of the building was enhanced by the large windows in the final bays of the north-east and south-west elevations and possibly in the gable ends as well. The late-14th century records refer to several payments for large windows. Some of these were probably glazed.

The interior of the Great Hall is another reminder of the sheer quality of the carpentry of the 14th-century guildhall. Tree-ring dating of the Great Hall timbers indicates that they were felled in *c*.1367. The bays of the Great Hall are separated by pairs of principal posts, each of which supports a slightly cambered, horizontal tie beam, with curved braces to the wall posts and cusped kerb principals. Above the tie beam on the first, third, sixth and seventh trusses of the Great Hall are 'crown post' trusses, with braced collars above. The timbers in the Great Hall tell us much about how the structure was actually erected on site, since they preserve the original sequence of carpenters' marks for the building. As with most timber-framed buildings of this period, the timbers for Trinity Hall would have been selected by knowledgeable carpenters in carefully managed woodlands. They would then have been transported to 'framing fields', probably on the outskirts of the city, where all the joints would have been pre-cut, before being transported and erected on-site. To

14th-century carpenter's marks on the timber.

enable the carpenters to match the timbers at the construction site, each was marked with a series of Roman numerals, scratched into the upper or 'fair' face of the timber with a race knife. To ensure that each pair of timbers was assembled correctly, the different sides of the building would be differentiated by marking one set of timbers with an additional line or 'kick'. An analysis of the surviving marks in the Great Hall indicates that construction commenced in the south-east gable end of the south-west aisle. It then continued down the south-west aisle to the screens passage bay, after which it returned up the north-east aisle to its dais end. Interestingly, the trusses associated with the northern end of the Great Hall are not marked within this sequence, suggesting that originally the Great Hall was intended to stop short of the screens passage bay, but that during the construction process it was decided to extend it further. We have noted above that this may well have been the limit of the earlier building on the site, and that at ground level, too, this end of the building differs from the remainder of the Undercroft.

Finally, it is important to think about the lighting and decoration of the Great Hall. The Great Hall would certainly have been darker than today. Two original windows are preserved in the north-west wall, and two more on the north-east wall are visible in the interior of the Great Hall. They would have allowed a much more diffuse and lower level of light to filter into the interior than their 18th-century replacements. Further light would have been provided by candles and rush lights, mounted on iron prickets inserted into the posts and timber rails of the Great Hall, evidenced again by surviving scorch marks. The infill panels in the Great Hall would have been whitewashed. Both the panels and perhaps some of the timber might have been stencilled and painted. A surviving panel on the north-east wall preserved evidence of a stencilled rosette design, which was perhaps a symbol of the Virgin to whom the fraternity was dedicated. The Great Hall was also decorated in other ways, with painted cloths and hangings such as the 'hallyng of pykture belonging to the hy deyesse' recorded in a 15th-century inventory. The Great Hall would also have contained furniture. The records refer to two 'bordes' and five trestles 'for the dece', which suggests that one or two long tables were provided for the Master and Wardens at the dais

end. Later records also refer to five 'mete bourdes for the south side with trestlles', with seven 'fourmes' or chairs and four 'mete bourdes of the north side of the hall'. This suggests that during feasts and meetings, members sat down the sides of the Great Hall, leaving room for servants and petitioners to move up and down the Great Hall, between the low and high ends. Other items of furniture related to the guild's business affairs included an iron-bound chest, which was purchased in 1436/7.

The kitchen

The permanent hospital community and the elaborate feasts held by the fraternity necessitated the presence of a kitchen. It is possible that this was located in the Undercroft, or in a building abutting the Great Hall. In 1432/3 the guild's records note payments for the construction of a clay 'rerdoes' in 'the kechyn in the Trinite halle'.

The Merchant Adventurers' Hall in the early modern period

In the early part of the 16th century, Trinity Hall continued to be used in much the same ways as it had been throughout the first two centuries of its existence. However, the Reformation had profound consequences for religious guilds such as the fraternity

This view of the Hall from the Fossgate entrance was painted by William Boddy in 1896 and shows the north-east range as it looked before the Governor's Parlour extension was built in 1949.

of Our Lord Jesus Christ and Trinity hospital. The guild's connection with the city's mercers saved it from suppression, unlike some of York's other religious guilds. Although trade had always been an important part of the guild life, during the 16th century this economic and political role became increasingly important, and gradually the guild transformed itself into the Society of Merchant Adventurers. Although the hospital also survived the Reformation, its charitable rather than its spiritual role became predominant.

The north-east range

These changes, not surprisingly, had an important impact on the medieval building. At some point in the late 16th or early 17th centuries the original entrance to Trinity Hall was transformed, first by the construction of the 'north-east range' and second by the reconstruction of the Gatehouse to Fossgate.

Classical motifs carved on the gables in the north-east range.

Today, the north-east range is the main point of entrance for visitors to the Hall. The date of this almost symmetrical, three-gabled, two-storey building with attics has always been a subject for debate. Detailed accounts do not survive for this period and, to date, no mention has been found in other records of its construction. Stylistic dating of the building is also difficult, due to its extensive restoration in the 1930s. However, close inspection of the building reveals surviving fragments of the original façade, including sections of the 'bargeboards' carved with Classical motifs such as scrolls and vineleaves around the gable roofs. Architectural records from the 20th century also indicate that there was an attempt to replicate what was being restored, such as the heavy entablature over the doorway into the Undercroft, which is carved with a frieze of arabesques, lozenges and lions' masks. The use of such Classical motifs parallels other examples found in the houses and public buildings in the city in

THE LOVING CUP CEREMONY

The Venison Feast held on 21 November 1952

Governor Christopher W. Rowntree begins the Loving Cup Ceremony. He faces the Lord Mayor of York, Alderman C.W. Wright, and drinks to him with the toast 'Bonne Aventure' whilst his back is protected by the guest to his left, Mr I.G. Rayden, Master of the Worshipful Company of Mercers. Seated next on the right is the Sheriff of York, Alderman F.W. Shepherd, also a Company member.

Those unfamiliar with the tradition of the Loving Cup Ceremony might be told that it dates back to 978, when the Anglo-Saxon King, St Edward the Martyr, was stabbed in the back whilst drinking from a goblet of welcome held in both hands whilst still mounted on his arrival at Corfe in Dorset. It can be a very confusing ceremony and no more than three people should be standing at one time. Indeed, this may be the only recorded occasion in the Company's archive when the drinkers are known to have actually got it right!

Although the ceremony only dates from the early 19th centruy and was widely used by the Livery Companies of the City of London, it did not arrive in York until the revival of the Venison Feast in 1951. The tradition continues today.

the early part of the 17th century. It therefore seems likely that the north-east range was built in the wake of the Society's newly granted charter of 1581.

One intriguing aspect of the building is that it also incorporates large amounts of re-used timber in its construction. This can best be seen along the north-west elevation. Here a series of carpenters' marks are visible, located where the principal posts and struts are morticed into the sill beam. These marks are also different from their medieval counterparts in being cut with a chisel, rather than a race knife and being set to the exterior façade of the building. The reason for this is apparent in the interior, in the modern-day office. Here, it is possible to see that the timbers making up this range are all re-used; covered with empty mortice and peg holes, cuts and scorch marks. The recycling of building materials might seem a very modern way of thinking, but it was common in a period in which timber was in increasingly short supply due to the disappearance of managed woodlands, and in growing demand not only in the construction industry but also in the shipping trade, in domestic heating and in newly emerging industrial processes. The shortage of timber was such that there was a re-used timber warehouse in the Jubbergate market of the city, where the timber may well have come from. In the middle room of the north-east range it is possible to identify a whole series of re-used common rafters, distinguished by their characteristic angled edges, which would once have sat on top of a wall plate and formed part of the roof of a medieval building.

It is impossible to be certain about the use of the north-east range during the late 16th or early 17th century. However, one important function of the

Lauren Marshall, Hall Manager, in the present-day office. Note the reused timbers in the background.

building was to provide a new, fashionable entrance and staircase to what must have begun to seem a rather old-fashioned guildhall. The remodelling of both the north-east range and probably the gatehouse entrance from Fossgate in the 17th century was a symbol of the new identity and status of the incorporated Company. The north-east range also provided Company members with a more flexible set of rooms which could have been used for a variety of functions: as meeting places, accommodation for guests and for storage of important documents and goods. The original appearance of the interior can best be seen at first-floor level, where four small rooms separated by stud partitions still survive today. The room to the north-west may have provided accommodation for a porter, as it still does today. Early 20th-century plans suggest there may have been a staircase connecting this room directly with the ground floor below. This space, now used as a kitchen, is also separated at ground-floor level from the remainder of the range by a partition.

The remaining three rooms on the first floor of the north-east range are well appointed. Each appears to have been heated by its own small chimney stack and may also have contained some form of stair or access to ground-floor level. The first room from the north-west also provides a stair to the attics above these rooms, which may once again have been used for accommodation or storage. Although the windows have all been replaced, they are likely to have been glazed casement windows, making these rooms seem much lighter than the dark guildhall beyond. Although the splendid carved fireplace now located in the Governor's Parlour is of 16th-century date, it is not an original feature of the room. It is said to have been removed from a house in nearby Pavement in 1925, and was installed in the room when the Company built the brick muniment room and ground-floor toilet range here in 1949. This house may well have been one part of the Company's extensive property portfolio centred around Fossgate, Pavement and Walmgate, or simply the house of one of its members. Either way it indicates that during the 16th century, members of the newly incorporated Merchant Adventurers were keen to demonstrate their connection to the Company in private as well as in public.

The Great Hall and Undercroft in the early modern period

Although the construction of the north-east range was the most significant and visible addition to the Merchant Adventurers' Hall in the early modern period, the medieval building was also transformed in subtle but important ways. The most visible change made to the exterior of the building was the plastering and whitewashing of the exterior, to mask the timber-framing which had been such an important symbol of the guild's medieval status and wealth. We know that the building was plastered because of the thousands of small, hand-made nails which were hammered into the surface of the principal posts and intermediate studs to receive and hold a plaster render and which are clearly visible today. Although the lack of survival

Arms of the Merchant Adventurers of England on the 16th-century fireplace.

THE CHRISTIAN BASIS OF THE COMPANY

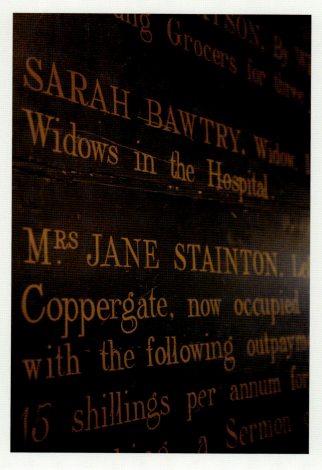

Jane Stainton's bequest is recorded on the Benefactors' Board in the Undercroft.

The medieval mind saw philanthropy as an end in itself, but there was also the entrenched belief that good works performed during a person's lifetime would have a beneficial effect as the departed soul travelled towards the heavenly kingdom via a stay of indeterminate length in purgatory. The hospital, the chantry altars, and care for almsmen and women were all part and parcel of this belief in the complete integration of life on earth and life beyond.

The Reformation did away with the concept of employing priests to say masses for the souls of the dead. But the Christian tradition of the Company lives on in various ways. Indeed, one of the six core purposes is to continue to uphold the Christian tradition of the Company whilst remaining open to all faiths and none. There is an annual carol service; at all feasts the Chaplain says Grace; there is a formal act of worship before the Charter Day Court and before the Michaelmas Feast. At his death in 1644 Sir Thomas Herbert, a member of the Company, left an endowment for a sermon which has been preached at the Michaelmas Service ever since. Jane Stainton similarly left money to endow an annual sermon which still takes place on 30 January in the church of All Saints Pavement as a memorial to Charles I.

of the plaster makes it difficult to say when it was applied, it is possible that this was part of an attempt to unify the appearance of the building during the 17th century.

Surviving accounts from the 1570s and 1580s suggest that there were also attempts to update and modernise the Great Hall. In 1571/2 and again in 1572/3, payments were made for the 'seallynge' of the Great Hall. The term 'sealing' is ambiguous. It may refer to the insertion of ceilings below the medieval roof trusses in the Great Hall. These ceilings largely survived until the early 20th century. But 'sealing' is a term also associated with wainscot or panelling, and so this record might refer to the installation of the wooden panelling which survives at the dais end today. The Hall was certainly still painted and

decorated at this period. In 1575/6 the accounts record expenditure on 'payntyng the marchantes Armes' in the Hall. This fascination with painting coats of arms, usually as a backdrop in front of which the most important members of the Company would sit, is found in two of the city's other guildhalls: the Merchant Taylors' Hall in Aldwark and St Anthony's Hall, which was shared by the City Corporation and the other craft guilds of the city.

There were other changes to lighting and heating in the Hall. New windows were added or old ones altered in 1504, but any traces of these were destroyed by the insertion of sash windows in the 18th century. A 'newe chymney at oure hall' was also created in 1574/5. This may well be the large, back-to-back fireplace and stack which survives in the south-west aisle of the Hall today, which was further altered in the 19th century. The same accounts record 'makyng Rowmes in the hall for lyeng of cloth'. This may well refer to the creation of the room today known as the Committee Room and suggests either that the Company were storing, or perhaps inspecting cloth and other goods in the Hall, rather than in people's houses, by this date.

In the Undercroft, it was probably the Chapel which was altered most as the Company sought to play down its religious origins. Fragmentary remains of an image of the Virgin and altar stones carved with the crosses representing the wounds of Christ were excavated in 1949. These may well have been damaged deliberately, as an act of iconoclasm, or more likely buried with the hope of recovering them should the religious policies of the Tudors shift back towards the old faith. Certainly, the multiple altars which were once the focus of masses and obits would have been removed with their associated statues. Windows would have been removed or whitewashed over and finally re-glazed with clear glass. In 1677 the Chapel was refurbished with the fixtures and fittings that survive today. It was probably at this date that the great east window was narrowed and one of the windows in the south-west wall removed; the other being re-set above the back of the new pews, as the roof was also raised. The original connection between the Chapel and the hospital may also have been severed by the construction of a partition wall between the Chapel and the remainder of the Undercroft. Early 20th-century plans show this partition in place, before it was removed in 1925. At some point a staircase also appears to have been constructed providing direct access from the dais end of the Great Hall to the Chapel entrance. The position of the stair is also marked on early plans of the building and you can still see the evidence for its position in a series of replaced joists at the south-eastern end of the north-eastern aisle of the Undercroft.

At some point in its history, possibly again during the later 16th or 17th century, the hospital was reorganised and subdivided into a series of separate rooms. Some of these were heated by the magnificent four-fireplace complex at the north-western end of the Undercroft. These partitions are also shown on the early 20th-century plans, prior to their removal in 1925. Evidence to support this is provided by Dr Maud Sellers's description of the 'oak studded and brick nogged partition running down the centre of

the hall'. The partitioning of the hospital suggests that it was changing its role, and becoming more like the almshouses being built by contemporary guilds and private patrons across England in the early modern period.

Display of three centuries of York silver in the Undercroft.

The Merchant Adventurers' Hall: 18th century

During the 18th century, the Hall continued to reflect the changing fortunes of the Company. One of the most significant changes made during this period was the insertion of sash windows into the Great Hall. In 1736 the York antiquarian Drake described the buildings as having been 'lately sashed' and in the same year expenditure was recorded on window shutters. It was probably during this century that the Great Hall was subdivided by a longitudinal partition into an 'inner' and 'outer' hall. The inner hall provided a comfortable meeting place, since the rooms in the north-east range were by this date being let to private tenants.

During the 18th century the Undercroft also functioned as a home to poor women. Only minor repairs were made to the Chapel and Undercroft during this period. In 1707 the minute book records a complaint about the repainting of the Chapel ceiling and in 1730 there was a request that the floor in the poor women's apartments should be raised, apparently as a result of flooding the previous year. Repairs to the Chapel were also made in 1797, with William Watson 'pointing in the new light in the Chapel window' and

Above: *Lunch for the German Ambassador in the Committee Room, March 2010.*

Right: *Roof timbers in the Great Hall.*

'pulling down a wall joining the Chapel, removing bricks and clearing of rubble'.

The Merchant Adventurers' Hall: 19th century

A plan of 1814 by the York architects Atkinson and Phillips provides a good snapshot of the layout of the building in the early 19th century. It shows the Hall divided into an 'inner' and 'outer' hall by a central partition. The present Committee Room was in use as a kitchen, and a 'soup room' occupied the sixth bay of the Great Hall. The buttery and pantry were in use as the 'Court of Assistants' Room' and the upper floor of the north-east range consisted (from north-west to south-east) of a tenement, a housekeeper's apartment and a boot house. Staircases are shown rising in the north-west and south-east of these rooms. The contemporary plan of the ground floor shows the Undercroft divided into a public room and into separate men's and women's apartments.

The most obvious change made to the appearance of the Merchant Adventurers' Hall during the 19th century was the removal of plaster ceilings and exposure of the medieval roof trusses. This process seems to have been initiated by an accident. In 1834 the *Yorkshire Gazette* recorded that 'one square of the ancient ceiling, about 9 feet by 7, fell down with a tremendous crash' in the north-east aisle while the Hall was being used for a Sunday School. Despite this incident it seems that the removal of the rest of the ceiling plaster in the Hall occurred slowly. The plaster was removed from the ceiling and elevation of the south-west aisle in 1892, and the re-exposed crown posts are visible on postcards from the turn of the century. Other areas of plaster were not removed until restoration work in 1925. In 1901 Alfred Proctor, the Governor, recorded that the 'the Hall was repaired and beautified' in 1833. Some of this work involved the refitting and repainting of the fireplace and judges' benches in the south-west aisle or 'inner hall', which survives to this day.

The Merchant Adventurers' Hall: 20th century

The Company's developing interest in its history and buildings was greatly enhanced by the work of their indomitable archivist, Dr Maud Sellers. From the 1920s the Hall began to fulfil an important educational role, and the archives of the Company contain files of letters of appreciation from visiting teachers and school pupils, although not surprisingly there was less enthusiasm for the introduction of entrance fees!

As the leisure and tourist industry began to develop in the city, the Merchant Adventurers' Hall increasingly became perceived as a 'heritage attraction'. The public hiring of the Hall as a venue for dinners, concerts and meetings of associations such as the White Cross Temperance Society (1901) and the Law Society (1949) also continued. More unusual events included an audience with Professor Tobin, the 'Great African Medicine Man', in 1909, the use of the Hall for a 'camouflage' event hosted by the YVRS in 1941, and the 1964–5 international women's table tennis championships.

Between 1920 and 1928 the first major restoration scheme in the Hall was carried out. Records of this work survive in the form of drawings, photographs and correspondence in the Company's archives, as well as those held in the Atkinson-Brierley collection at the Borthwick Institute for Archives in York. The work included restoration work to the south-east and south-west gables, the removal of the remainder of the ceiling plaster in the Hall, the removal of the partitions in the Hall and in the Undercroft, including the removal of the staircase providing access from the Hall to the Chapel, the reconstruction of 15th-century windows in the north-east wall of the Undercroft, the re-laying the floors in the Great Hall and Undercroft, the restoration and rebuilding of fireplaces, and work on the east gable. In addition, more than £2,000 was spent in 1925–6 on underpinning and other work in the Chapel. One of the more exciting events of this period was the rediscovery of original medieval windows in the north-west gable of the Hall, complete with surviving grooves for its original oak shutters. Drawings were made of the evidence and the windows were restored. The 1929 work also uncovered a section of plaster inscribed with initials and dates between what was referred to as the 'minstrels' gallery' over the screens passage and the Hall, although sadly, no traces of the gallery or the photographs survive today.

The involvement of the Society for the Protection of Ancient Buildings (SPAB) in restoration work of 1929 increased the appreciation of the national

significance of the Hall, as did its inclusion in the Ministry of Works' list of Scheduled Ancient Monuments in 1935. In many ways, much of the restoration of the 1920s involved the removal of the alterations made to the building in the 16th and 17th centuries, returning the building to its medieval appearance. Indeed, it is telling that in her description of the stripping of plaster from the north-east gable of the Hall, Dr Maud Sellers noted that it was being 'restored to its medieval aspect'. Important work on the Hall continued into the 1930s, and it was during this period that a fabric committee was established and 'appeal for funds' was launched. Contemporary photographs of the work indicate that many of the structural timbers and floorboards in the Hall and façade of the north-east range were replaced at this time. More medieval features also appeared during this work, including the surviving medieval windows and panel of plaster decorated with black and red rosettes preserved in the north-east wall of the Hall.

Restoration work on the Hall in 1938.

The post-war period: the 1947 scheme and after

The most important work of the post-war period was initiated in 1947 and continued into the early 1950s. The 'scheme of restoration' proposed by the Company architect J. Stuart Syme in 1947 resulted in the construction of a new range, providing toilet facilities at ground-floor level and a Governor's Parlour and strongroom above, and the Jacobean-style staircase which still connects the ground and first floors of the north-east range and provides visitors with access from the Hall to the Undercroft.

In 1954 there was an outbreak of dry rot introduced into the building via spores from the 1947 flood that left the Undercroft under 3 feet 4 inches of water. In 1967–8 the Chapel and Undercroft were again flooded. In 1974–5 the Hall was further improved by the

installation of a fire exit in the north-east corner of the south-east end of the Undercroft, and the installation of a system of emergency lights. At the same time the passageway entrance from the garden was closed off with railings because of the numbers of 'night visitors' who used the passages around the Hall for 'sleeping off the soporific effects of methylated spirits'.

In the early 1980s concerns about the structural condition of the building emerged. In 1982 the Undercroft flooded to a depth of nearly 4 feet 2 inches, causing damage to the Chapel pews and fittings. The floor of the Hall also appeared to be sinking, particularly near the chimney area at the rear of the Hall. Professional advice was sought and concluded that piling in Piccadilly, together with the effect of the flooding of the Undercroft, were to blame. In 1982–3 a building advisory group was established to review the conditions of the Hall. A three-year renovation programme followed, which comprised a survey of the timber frame by the architect F.W.B. Charles. Financial assistance was provided by a grant of £20,000 from the English Tourist Board. By 1985–6 the last phase of the programme, including the

Below right: Flooding in 1982.

Bottom right: The Hall has always been vulnerable to flooding. This picture of the chapel was taken in 1979.

Below: Staircase built as part of the 'scheme of restoration' in 1947.

THE VENISON FEAST

The great size and quality of the Merchant Adventurers' Hall in Fossgate clearly demonstrates its founding guild's need to accommodate great feasts. The earliest were probably held here in the mid-14th century, but all evidence for them is now lost. However, clues to their probable origins are provided by later documents. In 1572, for example, the accounts of Governor Christopher Herbert state that the pageant masters should collect the moneys required to stage the Company's annual feast, and make up any shortfall except for expenditure on venison and wine. This suggests that the early feasts were held by the Mercers' Company on the completion of their religious play or pageant, part of the famous cycle of York Mystery Plays.

Our first detailed knowledge of the content of a feast comes from an account probably dating from 1448. Like its successors, it is a random list of purchases and hired-in services, each with its respective price. This shows that the initial preparations included the purchase and grinding of 480lb of wheat ready to make pastries and loaves of bread. Extra fuel in the form of four skeps of charcoal and a load of brushwood faggots was brought into the Hall's kitchen, along with a supply of water, perhaps taken from the Foss. Having no permanent culinary staff, the Company then hired in a master cook, a number of spit-turners, a woman to scour and swill the pewter tableware, and someone to wash the tablecloths.

Since manners books of the period describe the order in which each dish was to be served, it is possible to re-assemble most of the remaining purchased ingredients into a reasonably accurate menu.

Excerpt from 1572 account roll showing the sum of 32s 10d received from the master and brethren for the Venison Feast: 'At our V[e] nyson Feast: receyvyd of the M[aste]r and Brethren of our Felloship beyng at oure venyson Feast appeyntyd by ouer holle compayny at our halle as in one partycler booke thereof mayd it doth appere the somme of xxxij s x d'.

Void *(of digestive sweetmeats)*
3oz sugar-coated aniseed (perhaps with further sugared spices), and spiced wine sweetened with some of 8lb of honey.

Many of these dishes were highly flavoured using 24oz pepper, 14oz ginger and cinnamon, 8oz mace and cloves, 2½oz of saffron, 10oz white sugar, 2lb dates and 2lb currants. Further relish was added by sprinkling 8oz of beaten 'drage' (a spices mixture usually including aniseed and coriander) over some of

The Venison Feast, November 1952.

First course
Pottage of beef stock, boiled beef from the Shambles, 21 capons, 72 fowls, 6 suckling pigs, venison accompanied by frummenty (stewed wheat), and perhaps fritters made with eggs, milk and breadcrumbs or flour.

Second course
Pottage of jelly made with 28 calves' feet (probably coloured with red sandalwood and yellow saffron), roast venison, 42 rabbits, 6 young herons, 2 partridges, 44 pigeons, 72 sparrows, probably small baked egg custards, jelly and fritters.

the dished foods just before serving. There would also be piquant sauces, such as mustard for the beef, ginger, mustard and salt for the heron, mustard and sugar for the rabbits, and ginger, vinegar and salt thickened with 'myying' bread for the pig and delicate venison.

Following the usual practice, the Company's principal officers and guests would occupy a top table, there to be ceremonially served with the finest foods, such as the herons, partridges, aniseed comfits and the famous York main bread. The ordinary members would sit at both sides of long cloth-covered tables down the length of the Hall, their food being dished communally for each 'mess' of four people, from which they could help themselves. To quench their thirst, 170 pints of wine and 416 pints of ale were ready to be poured into earthenware pitchers or coopered tankards and carried to the tables.

The expenses of this feast totalled £4 6s. 2d., to which the brethren contributed £2 0s. 11d., these sums approximating to £2,000 and £930 respectively in modern values. They would have been even higher had the venison been purchased, but it appears to have been donated by a wealthy well-wisher, as became usual. In 1472, however, the Company had to purchase three and a half does, a fawn and half a stag for £1 8s. 6d., about £640 today.

The Governor, Paul Shepherd, carves the first slice at the Venison Feast in 2009.

Similar venison feasts continued to be held through to the late 16th century, as may be seen from the following menu based on the accounts for 1590:

First course
Pottage of beef stock, boiled salt beef, roast beef, mutton and veal.

Second course
15 hens, 4 capons, 3 cockerels, 4 partridges, 30 fieldfares, 60 larks (most being roasted) and a baked turkey.

Void
Baked Warden pears (with sweetmeats).

Flavouring these dishes required 8oz pepper, 1oz each of cloves, mace and cinnamon, 3lb each of currants and raisins, 1lb prunes, 8oz dates, 12 lemons, and over 3lb of sugar. To accompany the main courses there were 228 pints of beer, 70 pints of claret and 12 pints of sack, while for the void there were 4 pints of mulled wine and 8 pints of muscatel and piment, the latter being a delicious dessert wine flavoured with numerous spices, herbs and honey. The total cost was £5 18s. 0d. Other Elizabethan feast accounts include payments 'to the players 10s' and 'to Robert Hewitt mussission (head of the York Waites) 3s. 4d.', showing that music formed part of the entertainment.

Such feasts lapsed in the early 17th century, being revived around the 1690s, only to lapse again after 1817. Presumably the Georgian feasts still followed the traditional form, gradually adopting the new dishes and manners of their day, but none of their detailed accounts have survived.

In 1951, the year of the Festival of Britain, that tonic for the nation designed to relieve decades of depression and war, the Merchant Adventurers held their first Venison Feast in 134 years. This proved to be so successful that it rapidly re-established itself as a major event in the Company's year. Now, every November, the members and their guests gather in their Hall to enjoy a feast of venison, spectacle and good fellowship, just as their predecessors did over 600 years ago.

The Company's Chaplain, the Rt. Revd David Smith, in the Chapel before the Charter Day Court in April 2010.

restoration of the Piccadilly frontage of the Hall, was complete and the repair of the Chapel was facilitated through a grant of £4,000, and £1,000 provided for information panels by the N.G. Terry Trustees. Further restoration work was carried out in the Chapel in 1996–7, where the wall plaster was stripped and replaced, and on the four-fireplace complex. In 2003 a major project was completed to make the Hall fully accessible including the installation of lifts and ramps and in 2009 a state of the art LED lighting scheme was installed in the Great Hall.

In 1944 a Trust Deed was drawn up for the maintenance of the Hall and the payment of pensions to decayed tradesmen of York or the contribution towards other purposes 'for the benefit of poor and deserving persons of the City'. In the post-war period the Company of Merchant Adventurers, like many other institutions, was inspired by the desire to rebuild England and to reinvigorate the spirit of community fostered by the Company. Charismatic individuals such as the archivist Bernard Johnson, the curator Cuthbert Morrell and the Governor Noel Terry inspired enthusiasm in others and it is no coincidence that under their auspices, the Hall played a key role in the opening ceremonies and processions associated with the Festival of Britain, on 3 June 1951.

'It is a fact of nature that as soon as a building is completed and ready for occupation, from that point of time natural forces combine to reduce the building to dust,' wrote Jack Birch, Past Governor and Honorary Surveyor, in the 1986–7 Annual Report. 'The time taken to achieve this result varies between different buildings, and on how well or badly the structure was built in the first place.' The 14th century was an era when the master craftsman reigned supreme, and John Craneby, the head carpenter in 1357, and his team employed many construction techniques, such as off-site fabrication for the complex roof structure that are considered new today. They did not need consultants, professional advisors or computer-aided design. Mechanical plant was unavailable, all materials were sustainable and transported by horse or barge to the site, thus giving a zero carbon footprint – the target for modern construction. Still in use after more then 650 years, the Hall is a splendid legacy of the craftsmen of the 14th century.

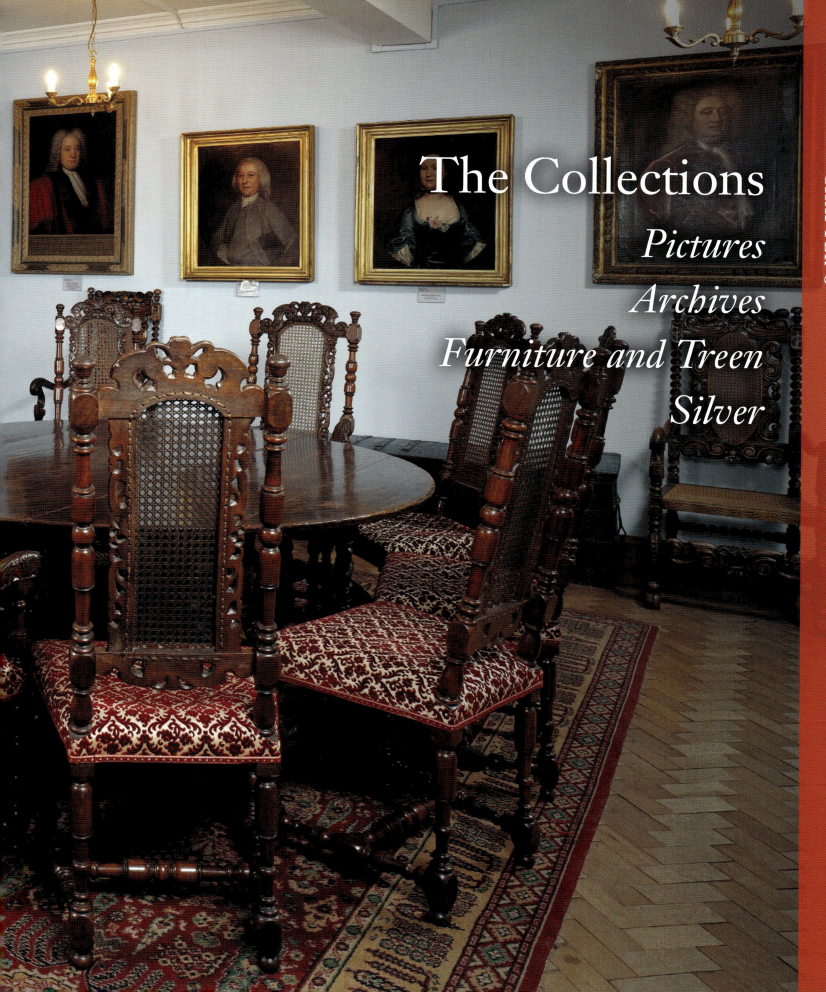

The Collections

Pictures

Archives

Furniture and Treen

Silver

The Collections: Pictures

The Merchant Adventurers' picture collection helps to tell the story of the Company. Portraits of former Governors predominate, looking down (usually benignly) on all today's activities in the Hall. The earliest portraits date from the time of James I or just before. There are three of these, and they give some idea of the activities members were engaged in at the time.

The earliest portrait seems to be that of William Wooller. He has a prominent handlebar moustache, and wears a ruff and a black doublet of improbable anatomical outline. Like most of the early portraits, his carries a painted inscription below, highlighting his charitable giving. From this we learn that 'By his last will 1597 did give 100 pound to be lent to twoo yong men Merchant Adventurers for three yeares and than to others accordingly for ever'. Such start-up loans appear to have been fairly common practice and it is interesting that the tradition has been revived in 2011.

On the left of the Governor's dais is William Robinson, an influential member of the York community, serving both as Lord Mayor and MP for the city (see box, p.47). The third early portrait has not been identified. It dates from about 1610, and is better painted than the other two. Under a black skullcap, above an elaborate ruff, a thoughtful face gazes out. The impression of seriousness is heightened by the book the sitter is holding, and by the presence of two skulls, one on his gold ring, the other an actual skull on which his right hand rests.

Moving further into the 17th century, more portraits survive in the collection. That of Stephen

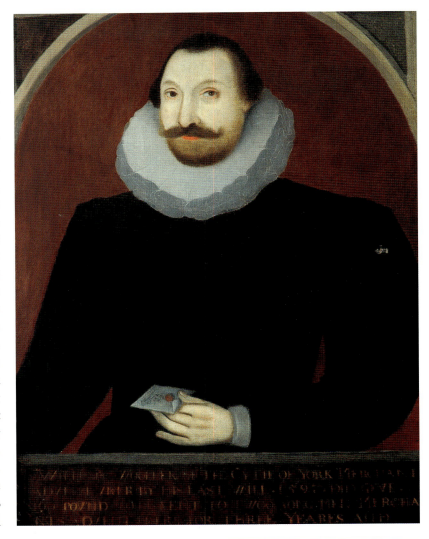

Previous pages: *The Governor's Parlour.*

Above: *William Wooller (Artist unknown, c.1600).*

Above: *Stephen Watson (Artist unknown, c.1660).*

Above right: *Unidentified man (Artist unknown, c.1610).*

Watson, a grocer who died in 1659, shows him wearing the traditional Governor's robe, almost identical to that worn to this day. It was also identical to the Lord Mayor's robe, which was convenient since many Governors filled that office too. Indeed, in between the robe's fur edging strands of the Lord Mayor's gold chain can be seen glinting. The inscription on Watson's portrait stipulates that the money he is bequeathing ('Threescore pound') is to be targeted specifically at 'young men Grocers'. A further inscription in Latin extols his generosity: *Laudant eum in portis facta eius* (His deeds praise him in the gates).

The portrait of William Hart (*see p. 35*) demonstrates even greater generosity as he gave '600 pounds to the companie of Merchant Adventurers to be lent to twelve young men exercising the same trade for two

yeares, and then to other twelve successivelie for ever – and also 300 to ye poore'. He takes us further into the history of the Company as much of his time was spent abroad. He was 'somtimes pastor of the English Church at Embden, and afterwards at Stode beyond the seas'. By 1622, after his time as Chaplain to the Merchant Adventurers overseas, he was back in York. For over a decade he gave large sums to alleviate poverty and also to be loaned out interest-free to different categories of Merchant Adventurers.

The portrait of Hart highlights a problem with many of the Company's early pictures. Left for centuries in an often cold and damp building, there are all sorts of condition problems. Hart is painted on a joined, quartered oak panel which has warped into a concave shape and split. There have been paint losses, and over-zealous cleaning has removed the word '*tempus*' from the phrase '*tempus fugit*' above the momento mori of an hourglass.

Several portraits from the end of the 17th century deserve mention. The rather sombre portrait of Michael Barstow is interesting because it highlights

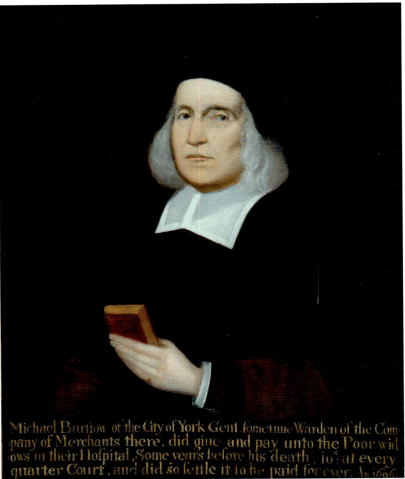

Michael Barstow of the City of York Gent. sometime Warden of the Company of Merchants there, did giue and pay unto the Poor widows in their Hospital, Some years before his death, 10ˢ at every quarter Court, and did so settle it to be paid for ever. Añ 1696.

Above: *Michael Barstow (Artist unknown, 1694).*

Left: *King George I, by Thomas Murray (1722).*

Sadly, no Governor chose to be painted by George Stubbs, who settled as a portrait painter in York for some years early in his career. With the city's strong support for the Hanoverians, it is no surprise that in 1722 a full-length portrait of King George I, 'his sacred Majesty', was presented to the Company by Thomas Murray and William Thomson. When the picture was cleaned in 1992, Murray's signature was found, so this has become the earliest portrait in the collection where the artist is known.

George I was not the earliest royal to be represented. That honour goes to Queen Henrietta Maria, whose portrait has pride of place at the far end of the Great Hall (*see p.45*). It is a variant on Van Dyck's picture at Windsor Castle, and was probably painted in the 18th century. For some time during the Civil War the Queen was in York, and it is recorded that she gave alms to alleviate the suffering of rebel prisoners who were being confined in the Hall.

the long association of some families with the Company. A later Michael Barstow was part of the Scarlet Pimpernel's team during the French Revolution, and the present head of the family, also Michael, was Governor in 1991–2.

The Georgian period produced several spirited portraits for the Hall but no masterpieces, and still only one portrait whose artist can be identified.

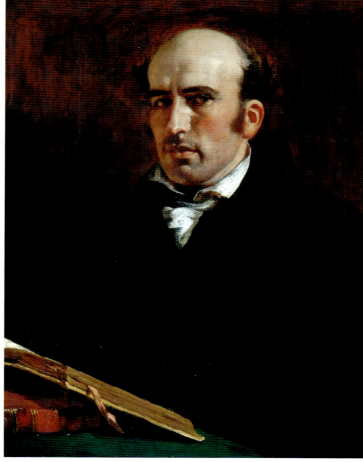

Above: *Lancelot Foster (Artist unknown, early 20th century).*

Above right: *John Francis Taylor, by George Fall (c.1848–1925).*

Right: *John Etty, by William Etty (c.1812).*

The portraits become more plentiful from the 19th century, and more is known about the sitters. There are, as expected, pictures of Governors who were prominent York citizens, and benefactors, like Lancelot Foster and John Francis Taylor. However, the finest portrait in the whole collection is not of a Merchant Adventurer but of a gingerbread maker, John Etty. Why the Company should have the picture is a mystery. It was painted by Etty's celebrated brother William in about 1812. Another portrait by Etty is that of John Thornton. Nothing was known of the sitter until a group of Merchant Adventurers spent some days in 2002 visiting Hamburg and towns of the Hanseatic League. Here they found that when Napoleon's army overran much of this area, John Thornton did his best to protect the property and interests of York Merchant Adventurers. One can speculate, therefore, that at some point after the Napoleonic wars John Thornton was able to visit

York, where his portrait was painted by Etty on one of the artist's frequent stays in his native city.

One of the earliest female portraits is a somewhat wooden depiction of Mrs Hardcastle (if the chalked name on the back of the stretcher is to be trusted). The painting is signed and dated 'Thomas Grimshaw 1850'. He was a York artist, working from a studio in Micklegate. Several more portraits by him can be seen in the Committee Room, including the large family group of the Wood family, who could be related to Mrs Hardcastle by marriage.

Four young members of the family are shown in this portrait in a landscape garden setting. Since the canvas bore the title 'The Wood Family' it was assumed to show four children of the Earl of Halifax, whose family name is Wood. However, recent research has proved that they are, in fact, members of the family of a prosperous pawnbroker from nearby Lady Peckett's Yard.

Top left: *John Thornton, by William Etty (possibly 1820s).*

Above: *The Wood Family, by Thomas Grimshaw (1850).*

Left: *Mrs Hardcastle, by Thomas Grimshaw (1850).*

Right: *Mrs Cook Cooper Taylor with her daughters (Artist unknown, c.1820).*

Far right: *Mr Cook Cooper Taylor with his sons (Artist unknown, c.1820).*

 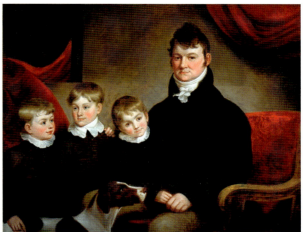

Flanking the Wood family are two other family groups, both of which have entered the collection fairly recently. They are in the style of John Russell and date to about 1820. On the right, Mr Cook Cooper Taylor, a York druggist, sits bolt upright, his three angelic young sons and the family dog standing by his side. The portrait next to him shows his wife and their two daughters. Husband and wife had been separated for about a hundred years until the Company purchased the male portrait, and accepted the females as a loan from The Royal Oak Foundation of New York.

However the most interesting picture in the room, albeit not the most decorative, is the canvas by another York artist, George Drummond, entitled 'Mr Hatfield showing samples of wheat'. The sitters, three of them wearing top hats, are all local men. Mr Hatfield, a York miller, wears a richly flowered waistcoat which contrasts with the sombre outfits of the other four. With a fine cloth he burnishes the grains of wheat. Money is on the table, and the scene may be taking place in a Corn Exchange, when the value of the crop is being decided.

Mr Hatfield showing samples of wheat, by George Drummond (c.1855).

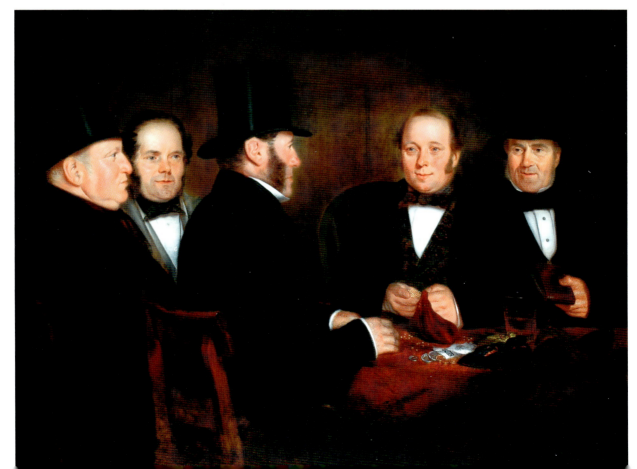

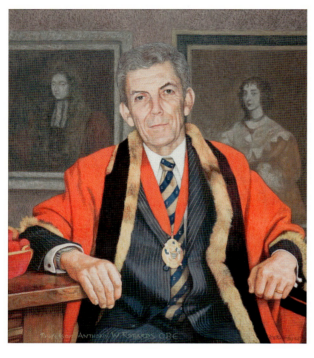

For much of the 20th century there are no portraits of members. It almost gave the impression to visitors that there were no longer any Merchant Adventurers. There are two portraits from the earliest years of the century but then a long gap until, in the 1980s, the newly appointed Honorary Curator of Pictures asked former Governors to consider having their portraits painted for display in the hall. A number obliged. A particularly fine portrait of the Company's Honorary Architect, Francis Johnson (Governor 1980–1), is by York artist John Langton.

Since then other Governors have been persuaded to bequeath their likenesses to the Company. The two most recent are of Professor Tony Robards (Governor 2008–9), painted by local artist Bob Brumby using the ancient method of tempera, and Paul Shepherd (Governor 2009–10) by the renowned portrait painter Andrew Festing.

However, as a break from tradition, a decision was taken in 2002 to commission a large group portrait, with each member who agreed to be included paying a proportion of the cost. The artist chosen for this

*Group Portrait
of the Company
of Merchant
Adventurers of
the City of York,
by Peter Mennim
(2003).*

mammoth task, Peter Mennim, had already painted a fine group portrait of the Merchant Taylors of York. The organisation of such an enterprise took many months. Individual appointments were made with the sitters, numbering roughly two-thirds of the membership. Many photographs were taken, and from these the artist selected a pose and arranged the grouping of figures. In spite of the fact that everyone is shown full face or in profile, the effect does not feel contrived, and all agree that individual likenesses are very well caught. A key to the names of those portrayed is placed alongside the painting, part of which is shown on the cover of this book.

Over the years other pictures have been given to the Company, though rarely are the names of donors recorded. Several are paintings of considerable artistic merit. A notable example is the large canvas hanging above the fireplace in the Hall. 'Old Ouse Bridge, York 1784' is by Joseph Farington RA, and it is thought to be the oil painting exhibited at the Royal Academy that year (*see p.33*). The view is taken from King's Staith looking upstream towards Lendal

Tower, seen through the old Ouse Bridge, with its picturesque buildings on either side. Figures and merchandise are on the quayside, and shipping on the river. This would have been a view well known to centuries of Merchant Adventurers, whose goods would have been loaded and unloaded on this very spot. Farington was told that he 'might leave this picture as his monument'. A smaller copy of the painting hangs in the York Mansion House, and there is a watercolour version too, as well as an engraving by Birch dated 1778.

Another oil painting of Old Ouse Bridge was purchased at auction by the Company in 2010. This is a much smaller composition, and is painted from the other side of the river (*see p.11*). Both views show the tower of ancient St William's Chapel, which stood at the approach to the bridge, where also was the Cloth Hall, used by York Merchants who belonged to the Eastland Company and the Merchant Adventurers of England. It was thought the painting might be by Edward Dayes (1763–1804). When it arrived at the Hall, and was being tried out in various locations, by a

141

remarkable coincidence a tiny picture hanging in the Undercroft was seen to be the print taken from this oil painting. Beneath the image is the artist's name: Edward Dayes.

One of the Company's finest pictures is 'Snow Scene with Skaters' by Jan Griffier the Elder, painted in the late 17th century. Griffier (1645–1718) was born in Amsterdam, but worked in London from about 1667 until his death, save for a visit to Rotterdam late in the 17th century. He was essentially a landscape painter, and was known for imitating the styles of more famous contemporaries. It is tempting to suppose that the picture was painted on his visit to Rotterdam, c.1695. The view is of a lively winter scene in a town. In the foreground figures skate on the frozen canal, and a finely caparisoned horse draws a sleigh. Spectral trees finger the dark sky. There are many buildings, some looking more like architectural capriccios.

Nearby hangs a painting of a sailing brig, *The Snow Studley*. The Curator of oil paintings at the National Maritime Museum wrote that 'the picture shows the *Snow* in three positions, about 1830, and sailing through the Downs. The artist is typical of a rising generation of ship portraitists.' A recent cleaning of the picture showed the name on the ship's pennant clearly as 'Studley'.

It would be interesting to know more about some of the other pictures in the collection like the late 17th–early 18th century Russian icon that was presumably brought back to the Hall by some merchant trading with Russia. Besides the Virgin and Child, the icon

shows four other figures. It was found rolled up in the attic by Patrick Waddington, a member of the Company, who paid to have it restored.

An interesting selection of smaller pictures can be seen grouped outside the Governor's Parlour. Some recent additions are by well-known artists, like the delightful night scene of the entrance to the Shambles by Cecil Aldin, or the same view by Dudley Hardy, whereas others are by local artists, who are now very well represented in the collection. One such is the 1876 sepia view of College Street by the quirky Victorian artist H. Waterworth, who always includes figures reminiscent of L.S. Lowry's some hundred years later. A number of the paintings here have been in the collection for a long time, notably the small watercolour of the English House in

Hamburg, signed and dated 'E. Gregorovious (18)47' (*see p.36*). This building, like the English Church in Hamburg, would have been a very familiar venue for York Merchant Adventurers, but whereas the church survived the war, the English House didn't.

So many of these local views have an added relevance to the Company as buildings and businesses shown in them are connected to Merchant Adventurers. A view of Stonegate by Nottingham

Above: *View of College Street, by H. Waterworth (1876).*

Far left: *View of Stonegate, by Rubens Arthur Moore (c.1884).*

Left: *Cecil Aldin's night scene of the entrance to the Shambles from King's Square (1935).*

Far left: *Walmgate Bar, by F. Bell (c.1850)*

Left: *Stonegate, by William Callow (1896).*

artist Rubens Arthur Moore is dated 1884. It is a finely detailed picture, so that even some of the items in shop windows can be identified, as can several of the shop signs. One (misspelt) reads 'Wadington', as these premises used to be where the noted piano-making firm of Waddington's was situated. The actor, Patrick Waddington, grandson of the founder of the firm, was a member. Opposite where this firm used to be is the outstanding half-timbered range of buildings called Mulberry Hall. Since the war it has been the famous china shop known by that name, founded by

the Sinclair family and now run by Adam who, with his father Michael, are both Merchant Adventurers. A larger watercolour of much the same view hangs nearby. It is by William Callow, signed and dated 1896, a remarkably dashing picture for an artist who was then aged 84. This was bought with a grant from the Victoria and Albert Museum, one of several bodies who have generously supported some of the Company's acquisitions.

For a long time the Company has accepted into its collection pictures of York. Several mid-19th-century

Artwork for a railway poster of troops crossing Lendal Bridge, by Fred Taylor (c.1925).

York Minster from the Walls above Precentor's Court, by Noel Harry Leaver (1889–1951).

watercolours of York buildings were painted by an amateur artist, F. Bell, and given to the Company by former Governor Thomas Bell. But for the most part the provenance of watercolours, as with oil paintings and prints, is not known. When the Company sought museum registration late last century, it was necessary to have an acquisitions policy. It was at this time that specific provision was made for collecting early views of York. Since then, many interesting topographical pictures have been acquired, both by gift and by purchase. A generous legacy from Past Governor Stephen Harland enabled the Curator to purchase some particularly fine watercolours. There is space to mention only a few of those here, to give some idea of the richness and variety of the Company's holding.

A large and splendid watercolour and gouache view shows troops crossing Lendal Bridge in about 1925, probably on their way to fire a royal salute in the Museum Gardens. This powerful image was painted by Fred Taylor RI, the noted railway poster artist, and is his original artwork for one of the exceptional posters he created to promote travel to the city.

Also on display is an exquisite watercolour by Noel Harry Leaver, an artist better known for his views of the Near East. In his depiction of the Minster from the Walls above Precentor's Court he has excelled himself in capturing the scene on a Spring day. The impression of sunshine on a breezy day is expertly conveyed. The view is interesting for showing what this area looked like before the vast bulk of the Purey Cust Nursing Home swept away the ancient foreground properties.

The final picture bought with the Harland legacy is one of the smallest in the collection. It is a watercolour by

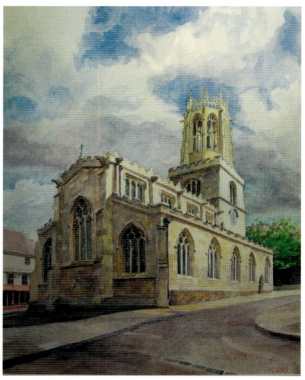

Albert Goodwin, friend of Ruskin and a prolific painter. Goodwin is an exciting artist as he often experiments with unusual views or scenes caught in a spectacular light. In his painting of the Minster taken from the Walls above the garden of Gray's Court, he daringly chooses to depict his subject very late on a summer evening, when hardly any natural light is left. At first glance you see just a very dark image, but then your eye begins to explore, first noticing a single light in a downstairs window, then spotting figures moving along the garden path between beds of tall white flowers, and finally tracing the outline of the Minster against the dark sky.

Other recent purchases hang in the Governor's Parlour and the anterooms. A watercolour of All Saints Church, Pavement, by F.W. Booty and dated 1917, was the first picture to be acquired showing the Guild Church. Since then a fine modern watercolour of the church from a different angle, by Mark Kesteven, has been added, and also a Victorian watercolour illustrating the church rising above ancient buildings long since demolished.

Some very interesting watercolours, all by the same hand, hang in the Committee Room. They form a series of 15 views of the city, painted in 1835 by

Above left: York Minster from the Walls, by Albert Goodwin (1845– 1932).

Above: All Saints Church, Pavement, by Mark Kesteven (2009).

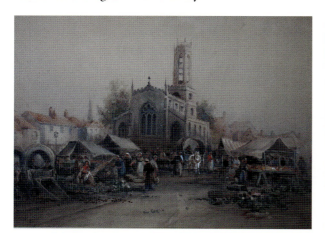

Far left: The market on the Pavement, with All Saints Church in the background, by F.W. Booty (1917).

Left: York Minster from St. Leonard's Place, by Charles Dillon (1835).

Above: *Houses next to All Saints Church, North Street, by George Nicholson (c.1825).*

Right: *Houses in Goodramgate, by Henry Cave (c.1812).*

an artist signing himself C. Dillon, about whom very little is known. A family of that name was in business in the city at the time, and the collection also has a fine panoramic print of York by one Charles Dillon. The watercolours, though clearly the work of an amateur, are unique in that they give a more comprehensive view of what the city looked like at the end of the Georgian era than in any previous period. In less than ten years the first photographs would be taken in York streets and this would revolutionise the accurate depiction of the historic city. Dillon's charming views are teeming with life: there are soldiers, gardeners, men in smocks; chimneys belch forth smoke; cattle are driven through the streets; overloaded stagecoaches rumble by; people look in shop windows or pop into taverns; and there is even a crowded paddle steamer on a trip past Bishopthorpe Palace. Details such as shops and inns are faithfully reproduced, so we can be sure of the accuracy of the views, even if Dillon has only a poor sense of proportion. His people are sometimes drawn much bigger than the horses transporting them.

The Company is fortunate to have another, smaller series of watercolours of York scenes. The artist, George Nicholson, was a professional and his views are painted about ten years before Dillon's. He uses an attractive palette of soft, warm colours with a dark reddish-brown line to delineate certain features. An aspect of his work is to exaggerate the picturesque

147

nature of the properties he is depicting. In this he is following the lead of York artist Henry Cave, whose *Picturesque buildings in York sketchd & etchd by H. Cave* was published in London in 1813. The plates in Cave's book record, and often exaggerate, the quaintness of early architecture in York, and thus whilst according with the new fashion for the picturesque, the book was also a forerunner in heralding York's tourist potential. The Company has recently acquired one of Cave's drawings from his book. It is of great interest in showing how faithfully Cave's etchings followed the details in his drawings, even down to the knots shown in woodwork, but with one exception. Whereas the drawing of ancient properties in Goodramgate shows a plain Georgian house to their left, Cave has decided to alter this in the print to a quainter building with lattice windows.

Mention must be made of the prints, many of which adorn the entrance to the Undercroft. These range from some of the famous early panoramas of the city, like the 'South-East Prospect' by Samuel and Nathaniel Buck, to a variety of smaller prints and etchings. There is an entertaining set of four prints showing the interior of the Minster during the hugely successful music festivals of the 1820s. These were produced locally and were clearly a rushed job as various blotches and back-to-front lettering show. The structures built to hold the vast crowds who attended look alarming to a generation used to health and safety regulations.

The Company also possesses a small number of drawings. Prominent among these are the beautifully detailed views of the Hall by a York man, Edwin Ridsdale Tate (1862–1922). He studied at the York School of Art before going to London to work as an architect. When he later settled in his native city, he specialised in the restoration of ancient buildings. Ridsdale Tate's output of drawings was prodigious, and many were used as book illustrations, as were some on display here. He was especially good at imagining scenes of how the city might have looked in the past, and his great panorama of York in the 15th century is justly famous. His meticulous pen-and-ink studies line the walls of the entrance staircase. They include what is possibly the best-known view of the interior of York Guildhall before its destruction in the war, and also an intriguing prospect for how the garden at the Hall could be laid out. This presumably was drawn at a request from the Company when the ramshackle outbuildings which used to cover the site were cleared away in the early 20th century.

The character of the Merchant Adventurers' Hall is enhanced by its collection of pictures. Most are relevant in some way or other to the Company and its history, and the acquisitions policy now ensures that all new additions adhere to these guidelines. The collection is growing steadily, and this trend is likely to continue, especially since the Hall is the only place in the city where there is a sizeable assembly of early York views permanently on display.

Opposite: *The entrance to the Hall, by Edwin Ridsdale Tate (1862–1922).*

Below: *Print of South East view of York, by Henry Cave (1803).*

The Collections: Archives

The notable continuity of ownership and occupation of the Merchant Adventurers' Hall has been reflected in the survival of its archive. Not only does it contain the sealed document in which, on 16 December 1356, William Percy granted to John Freboys, John de Crome and Robert de Smeton 'all that plot of land with all its buildings and appurtenances lying in the neighbourhood of Fossgate, in York; in width between the land called Trychour Lane on the one side and the River Foss on the other side, and extending in length between the king's highway of Fossgate in front as far as the land of Henry de Haxiholm at the back' (*see p.10*), it also contains a series of deeds dating back to 1301 which relate to the same plot of land, showing how it changed hands several times between various tradesmen and mayors of York before the guild in honour of our Lord Jesus Christ and the most Blessed Virgin Mary acquired it to build its Hall. Account rolls from the 1350s to 1366 record the purchase and carriage of building materials and the hire of workmen; there are receipts of money and gifts from members, including such items as a silver cup and a maple-wood drinking bowl holding half a gallon. Payments to lawyers, legacies, and rents were noted, and 8d. to a clerk for copying a charter and writing a release. We are reminded of the important part played by the guild not just in its members' lives but also in their deaths by a note of the costs of candles

Left: *The 1581 charter.*

Below: *The cartulary of the Mystery of Mercers.*

for burning around the bodies of deceased members. Then as now, meals and feasts took place, including one costing 6s. 8d. which was given 'for many widows' in 1366–7.

Although the Company does not hold a copy of Edward III's licence to found a guild, granted in 1357, it does have a copy of the charter granted by Henry VI in 1430, which incorporated the Mystery of Mercers of York and gave it the power to elect a governor and two wardens. Queen Elizabeth I's charter of 1581 incorporated the Mystery of Mercers as the Company of Merchant

Adventurers of York, in response to the 'decay and poverty' of the merchants. This bulky document bears a large royal seal showing the enthroned Queen on one side and the monarch riding a horse on the other (*see p.42*). One of the glories of the archive is its large number of medieval charters recording property transactions dating from the late 12th century. Most of these properties were in York and many of the deeds still bear seals, which have been photographed but so far have not been published. In the 15th century, for safe-keeping and ease of access, most of the charters were copied into the cartulary, which also contains copies of charters not found elsewhere in the archive and a list of brethren and sisters admitted between 1420 and 1495.

There have been losses from the archive, notably during the late 16th century and the 17th century. During the Civil War the Hall housed soldiers, prisoners from both sides and even ammunition; the upheaval caused by these events alone, apart from the disruptions of war and divided loyalties of members, may have caused irretrievable damage, destruction or dispersal of records. The cartulary itself was lost in about 1730, but in 1890 it was found in the

library at The Oakes, in Derbyshire. One can only speculate how it got there, but it was not unknown for antiquarians to borrow books they wished to study or copy. Once out of the Company's hands it may have been forgotten, lent or lost; the cartulary was eventually returned to the Company in 1917. It is because of such losses that modern archives rarely release material, except for public exhibitions such as the one at York City Art Gallery in 2010, when the Company lent its pageant inventory and bond for an exhibition celebrating the York Mystery Plays. The inventory is a detailed record of the props used for the 1433 performance of *The Last Judgement*, performed each year by the Mercers Company. It was published in the *Records of Early English Drama*, and its puppet angels, rainbows, clouds, not to mention the moving

Right: *Inside the archive.*

Far right: *Seals for the 20th-century grant of arms.*

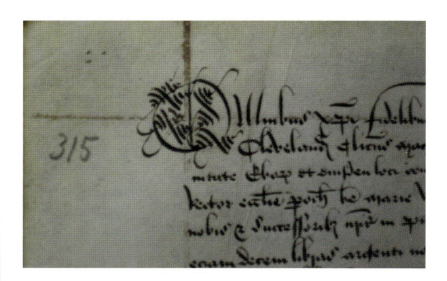

parts, curtains and hell mouth, bring to life the medieval performance of the wagon play.

The Company's medieval records have been studied in depth, notably but not exclusively by its archivists Maud Sellers, Louise Wheatley, Bernard Johnson, David Smith and David Palliser. In 1907 the Company decided to pay Maud Sellers a sum 'not exceeding' five guineas for preparing a prospectus for the publication of Company records, and the completed book was published by the Surtees Society in 1917. Her interest in the documents raised awareness in the Company of their importance and she became the company's first archivist in 1918. Apart from a gap of seven years between Dr Sellers' death and the appointment of Bernard Johnson, the Company has now had an honorary archivist for nearly a hundred years, and since 2002 an assistant archivist, Dr Jill Redford, has been employed for four hours a week to manage the day-to-day running of the archive.

Bernard Johnson, archivist from 1946 to 1975, was a Company member and governor whose papers show his energetic care for the archive; he employed his own secretary to write to would-be visitors, would borrow archival papers for visitors to examine at his place of work and resigned his post on one occasion over the question of the security of the strongroom. He successfully traced several lost archival documents and his deep interest in the Company's history was reflected in his lengthy contributions to the Company's annual reports and his two published monographs, *The York Residence of the Company of the Merchant Adventurers of England* and *Church of England, Hamburg*.

Above: *Decorated letter 'O' from the cartulary.*

Left: *Part of an account roll dating from the Feast of the Assumption 1366 to the Feast of the Assumption 1367.*

Dick Reid was Governor 1993–4 and Honorary Archivist 1975–88, and his annual curatorial reports demonstrated his interest in all aspects of the building and its contents. In 1976 he was able to report that the University of Toronto had paid for the microfilming of the Company's pageant documents, and the cartulary was microfilmed soon afterwards. The microfilming of the archive continued for at least 15 years with the aid of various grants. Dick Reid was instrumental in acquiring many of Bernard Johnson's books and pamphlets for the library and in producing publicity material for the Hall. His discovery of plans of the Hall dated 1814, published in the annual report for 1981/2, showed that what is now the Committee Room was then a kitchen, with an adjacent soup room, and that the men's apartments in the hospital in the Undercroft were situated where the present archive office now exists. In the same report he referred to the fact that the Undercroft had flooded twice in the last three years and his photograph of the flooded interior of the chapel showed just how severe the problem was (*see p.127*).

Professor David M. Smith, who was Director of the Borthwick Institute for Archives while acting as the Company's honorary archivist (1988–98), produced the invaluable *Guide to the Archives of the Company of Merchant Adventurers of York*. In his introduction to

this work he outlined and acknowledged the efforts of former Company members and archivists in listing the contents of the archive, as well as noting some recent losses. He oversaw the conservation of several of the Company's medieval documents and also prepared photocopies of many of them for study at the Borthwick Institute. He produced a list of members for the years 1581–1835, which the assistant archivist has supplemented with a list for the period from 1836 to the present day; in 2010 these combined lists contain the names of just over 2,200 people, a number which will be increased when a full list for the period 1357 to 1581 is completed.

Dr Louise Wheatley (1999–2000) made extensive use of the Company's records in her MA and PhD theses, and in doing so created a valuable biographical register of members in the 15th century. She also encouraged visits to the Hall by educational groups, a tradition which is still maintained.

David Palliser (2001–8), Professor Emeritus of Medieval History at the University of Leeds, presented the archive with, among other things, his transcription of about two-thirds of the cartulary, originally produced for a publication which did not reach the press. He also wrote the very popular *Company History* booklet, which visitors have been able to buy since 1985. Rita Freedman, former archivist at York City Archives, succeeded Professor Palliser in 2008, and has instigated the cataloguing of the entire archive.

Other researchers who have made use of the archives include Dr Kate Giles in her archaeological study of York's guildhalls, and a local group, The Latin Project, which published an edition of five early account rolls in 2007 and is now working on the account book dating from 1358 to 1369. A local historian, Anna Bissett, transcribed a set of 22 letters written to a colleague in Konigsberg by James Hutchinson, a Company member and a merchant in Danzig in 1646 and 1647 which, apart from their intrinsic interest, survive from a period when other archive papers are relatively scarce (*see box, p.16*). Recent studies have been made of the Company's role in the foundation of the York dispensary (founded 1788) and the York Chamber of Commerce (founded 1895).

There are areas of the archive which have been relatively under-used, and they include six minute books in the archive dating from July 1677 to April

Cartulary, fos.60v–61r; showing entries for Fossgate.

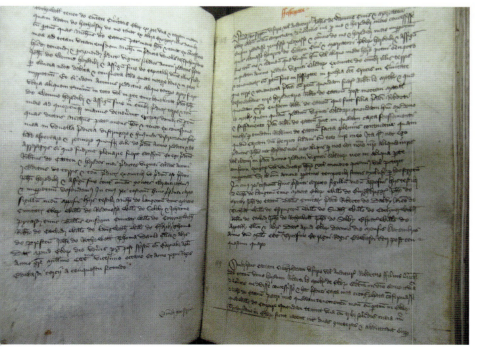

Far left: Seal on charter dated 1328, Henry son of Elias le milner of Swinton granting land in Jubbergate to Nicholas son of John de Appelby.

Centre: Seal on charter dated 1327, John Curteys granting land in Peter Lane Little to Alan de Furnes and his wife.

Left: Seal on lease of land in Goodramgate granted by the Guild of Holy Trinity Fossgate in 1503/4.

1985. Although they drily record attendances and absences from meetings, the election of officers, the admission of new members, and the overseeing and scrutiny of loans made from Company funds to young merchants, the long period of time which they cover gives a considerable amount of information about the running of the Company and those matters which interested it. The minutes for this period also provide an insight into the running of the hospital in the Undercroft, and show how people applied for places in the hospital or other charitable help.

The arrangement of the medieval archive is not known; surviving account rolls bear combinations of letters for ease of identification, while the charters were originally folded, with a Roman numeral and a note of the donor written on the outside. The different sets of documents may have been stored in bags or boxes before being placed in the Company's medieval evidence chest. Some medieval archives used cupboards with labelled pigeonholes or drawers and a similar arrangement may have existed at the Hall in Fossgate. Before the appointment of Maud Sellers, the custody of Company records appears to have been shared by company officers and employees, and 19th-century minutes contain many entries recording that the new Governor has taken possession of the Company's charter in its mahogany box, while other papers were entrusted to the Wardens. In 1850, a book of acts and ordinances, the new minute book and an apprenticeship register were said to be kept in the State Room Closet, presumably in the care of the Clerk or other officers. In about 1951 a strongroom was built for the archive, but the expansion of the

Company's more modern records resulted in an overflow into the adjacent muniment room and in 2003 increasing demand for office space resulted in the creation of a small office in the Undercroft for the storage of these later records. This room is partly below ground level and prone to continual damp; in 1947 flood water in the Undercroft had reached a level of one metre (39½ inches), a level which, if ever repeated, would submerge the archivist's computer and the two lowest shelves of documents. While the Company has prepared contingency plans for such an event, improvements to the River Foss, as the floods of 2000 showed, have made this an unlikely occurrence and a continually running dehumidifier controls the moisture levels on a day-to-day basis. The Undercroft room is fast becoming filled by the paper records, photographs and digital material produced and acquired by the Company in the 21st century.

Original binding of minute book for 1795–1846.

Minute book 5, for 1908–51.

Family historians provide most of the enquiries made to the archive, but there are also enquiries and visits from academics who are researching aspects of local or national history, although restrictions of space and staff mean that visits to the archive have to be limited.

The archive, like the Hall and the members who support it, is adapting to the digital age. A shortened version of Smith's *Guide to the Archives* is available on the Access to Archives (A2A) website, a database of archive catalogues in England and Wales which can by searched by anyone with internet access. Since 2010 the issue of creating digital images of its contents for reference and security has been addressed, together with the need for a fully comprehensive catalogue of every item although, as for most archives, identifying these objectives is easier than finding the resources to achieve them. The varied nature of the modern archive, with its letters, accounts, plans, photographs, tape recordings, and digital images and records requires different forms of preservation, not least the requirement to update computer software and storage systems. While, given a knowledge of Latin and palaeography, a 14th-century charter can still be handled and understood, information held on a floppy disk made only ten years ago would already be difficult to access.

Apart from the accumulation of Company records, the archive also contains other items. Some members have handed over collections of correspondence and memorabilia acquired during their time in the Company, while others have made gifts of books and documents. Some of these are in the archive's small library which contains several books concerning guilds, trade, and various aspects of the history of York. There is a collection of magazine articles about the Hall and the Company, and the archive also holds a collection of newspaper cuttings.

As the building has changed and grown, so has the collection of documents within it. With an archive reaching back more than 700 years, the Company is grateful to those who wrote and preserved all those documents and is keenly aware not only of the value of even seemingly insignificant documents, but of the responsibility owed to future generations to preserve and maintain today's records. As Louise Hampson, former archivist at York Minster, has said: 'Archives tell us who we are, where we have come from and how we got to where we are; they are the route maps of our past'; in spite of wars, floods, and the inevitable accidents of time and the actions of men, the Merchant Adventurers' archive has survived as a product of over six centuries of activity, and of pride in the Hall and in the community.

For any archivist, the security of the collection is of the first importance. It is achieved not just by protection from fire, flood and mice, but in knowing what an archive contains and where to find it and keeping a collection in such a way that it is not casually dispersed and moved around. This involves effort and expense and perhaps it is fitting to end this contribution with another quotation: 'The possession of great riches involves corresponding obligations, and the fact that we pride ourselves on a fine collection of documents means that we must take measures for their care and preservation beyond the span of one life' (Bernard Johnson, Annual Report 1950–1).

Dr Jill Redford in the Hall archive.

The Collections: Furniture and Treen

The extensive Company archive makes only four references to furniture and nothing after 1450. The 1435 account roll lists an iron-bound oak kist. These accounts also list keys for locks. This is undoubtedly the 15th-century kist or chest at present in the Governor's Parlour. Later account rolls list oak boards, trestles, a cupboard, a bed, and two iron chests which remain. The Company has no other furniture from prior to the 17th century, after which the present furniture and fittings were acquired, gifted or loaned.

The principle furnishing is the early 18th-century Governor's Stall in the Great Hall. No minutes or account entries have yet come to light on how it came to the Hall. Substantial, well designed, it is believed to have been made for the Burlington Law Courts as the Judges' seat with a Sheriff's seat to left and right for the sheriffs of the City and the Ainsty. This Court was demolished in the 1780s to make way for John Carr's new Law Courts. It was moved to the Cloth Hall on Ouse Bridge and used by the Merchants at that time. Legend has it that it was moved to the Hall when the new Ouse Bridge was built about 1812.

Above is the carved and illuminated Company Arms designed by Francis F. Johnson (Governor 1980–1) and Dick Reid (Governor 1993–4) who carved it in 1971. Prior to that date the Company used the arms of the Merchant Adventurers of England which can be seen in a painting of 1669, now in the Chapel, as well as on one of the banners hanging in the Undercroft. The late Past Governor Bernard Johnson was an heraldic enthusiast who was determined to see the Company have its own

Above: *Dick Reid, centre, helps carry the coat of arms, carved by him in 1971, into the Hall.*

Left: *Chest or 'kist' purchased by the Mercers' Guild in the early 15th century. Once used to store documents, it is now in the Governor's Parlour.*

arms. He duly applied to the College of Heralds who granted these arms in 1971. They differ slightly from the arms of the Merchants of England, for instance there is a white rose of York depicted on the wings of each supporting Pegasus.

The idea at the time was to have the arms resting on the pediment of the stall. This could not be achieved satisfactorily so the arms were modified by taking away the field on which arms usually sit, and the ribbon and motto were contrived in such a way to make a more jewel-like arrangement which could be raised above the stall. The ribbon was duly painted red to balance the cold colours of the arms themselves. The arms were carved in Quebec yellow pine, laminated to give a relief of six inches, then gilded and illuminated.

The other major fitting is the seating in the Chapel which dates from the late 17th century. The altar table of similar date came from St Margaret's Church, Walmgate, in the 1980s. The gilded altar cross and candlesticks, again by Francis F. Johnson and Dick Reid, date from the 1970s.

Upstairs the three anterooms lead into the Governor's Parlour. These rooms contain 17th-century oak armchairs, chests, bible boxes and a rare child's high

Above: *The coat of arms above the Governor's stall in the Great Hall.*

Right: *Gilded altar cross and candlesticks in the Chapel.*

chair. The third room has two interesting chairs. In the 12th century wood turners were some of the first stool and chair makers. Over the centuries the turned chairs became grander and grander with elaborate backs, arms and wings. This 18th-century turned armchair, sometimes called an 'Abbot's Chair', is a fine example of the turner's craft and about as grand as they come. The 20th-century oak chair carved by 'Mousy Thompson' of Kilburn has a high back. Carved near the top are the Company's (old) arms with the mouse on the beading; it is known as the Governor's chair and is used by the Governor on Company occasions.

In the Governor's Parlour the double gate-legged walnut table in the 1680s style is the centrepiece of the room, surrounded by eight high-backed walnut chairs of the same style. The room is dominated by the 16th-century oak chimney over-mantel carved with birds and mythical beasts and the arms of the Merchant Adventurers of England in the centre. The room has a mid-18th-century long-case clock by Jon N. Storr of York in one corner, and one of the Company's ornamental carved and illuminated maces between the windows.

The Company's main processional mace dating from 1722 usually stays in the Chapel. Originally Sheriff Robert Deglew's staff of office, it was redecorated with the old Company's arms in the 19th

century and presented to the Company by the then Governor. The mace rests on the south wall of the Chapel and has two interesting dates – above 1707, and below 1801. It is not certain what the dates signify but they are the same as those of the Union of the Scottish and English Parliaments in 1707 and the Scottish and English with Northern Ireland in 1801.

Above left: *Carved and illuminated mace in the Governor's Parlour.*

Above: *Main processional mace (1722).*

Far left: *Carved mouse on the Governor's chair.*

Left: *Carved furniture in the anterooms leading to the Governor's Parlour.*

Below left: *The Governor's Parlour.*

Opposite: *18th-century turned armchair.*

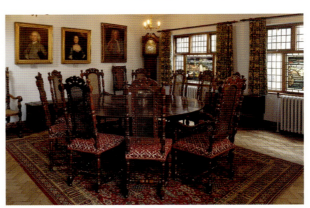

The Collections: Silver

Despite tantalising references in the archives to gifts of silverware – a 'cup made of silver' from Peter Potter in 1358, a 'cup with a cover and six spoons' from the Kelsterne family in 1362, and to silver in the 15th century for the three altars of the chapel – such plate has long since been dispersed, and the only survival original to the Company prior to 1900 is a beautiful tall goblet made in London by Walter Shute (c.1635), engraved on one side with the arms of the Merchant Adventurers of England, and inscribed on the base: 'Guift of Mathew Topham. Alderman of this Citty to the Company of Merchants who deceased the last day of Ja 1635.' Topham was admitted into the Company in 1598, becoming Governor in 1620.

Notwithstanding this one survival, today the Company has a notable collection of plate, much dating back to the 17th century, accumulated largely in the 20th century through the generosity of members and their families who have gifted silver for use on formal occasions in the Hall and in the Chapel.

Below left: Goblet by Walter Shute (London c.1635)

Below: Thistle shaped goblet by Martin Barber and William Whitwell (York 1821).

Right: *The 'pegs' inside the 5-peg tankard by Thomas Mangy (York, 1675).*

Far right: *Double Pomegranate Thumb Piece on 4-peg tankard by George Gibson (York 1675).*

Below: *Elizabethan Communion Cup (1568).*

The nucleus of the older pieces comes from a collection of early York silver formed by William Riley-Smith, the Tadcaster brewer and member of the Company and sold by auction in 1952. The Directors of Rowntrees, several of whom were members of the Company, acquired two pieces for presentation to the Company: one, a rare 'cannon ended' spoon dating from 1680 and the other a magnificent 'peg' tankard of a design particular to the North of England. With a plain cylindrical body mounted on three pomegranate-shaped feet and a hinged cover having a double pomegranate thumb-piece, it was made in 1675 by George Gibson, a well-known York craftsman. Such tankards were designed for communal use to be passed around the table; inside are inset pegs used as markers of individual measures.

Those items which failed to sell at Riley-Smith's sale passed to his son William, also a member of the Company, who in his will most generously gifted them to the Company. Thus came to Fossgate no fewer than ten items, the majority dating from before 1700. An

Cannon-end basting spoon by John Thompson (York 1680).

Wine Cups (York c.1680).

Elizabethan communion cup and cover dated 1568 is the most important piece, together with a plain-sided tankard of 1684 by William Busfield, a two-handed 1659 wine taster by William Waite, a 1666 wine cup by Thomas Mangy and a number of small Charles II tumbler cups used as personal drinking vessels.

Further presentations of early York silver were made by Noel Terry (Governor 1935–6) of a plain-sided 'peg' tankard of 1667 by Thomas Mangy; an unusual silver-mounted coconut cup by William Busfield (c.1690) given by Robert Tetley in 1967; and an attractively decorated two-handled porringer of 1682 by George Gibson, donated in memory of Gilbert Johnson (Governor 1933–4).

The Company has thus acquired an important collection of early York silver, to which has recently been added an elegant Charles I wine cup by Francis Bryce, hallmarked 1636–7. It is the earliest example of York-made domestic hollow-ware so far recorded, in pristine condition, and purchased in 2008 by subscription and with the support of the Goldsmiths' Company and other trust funds.

Silver from the 18th and 19th centuries is largely represented by presentation wine cups and goblets, of which the Company has no fewer than ten examples. The highlight of the Georgian collection however is a magnificent venison dish made in York in 1810 by Robert Cattle and James Barber. Presented in 2009

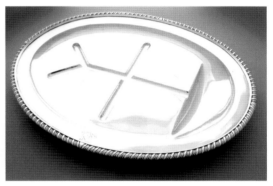

by Governor Paul Shepherd and his Lady, Virginia, for use at the Venison Feast, the dish stands on two ball feet at one end and has four channels which run into a well at the other end. It is the only York-made example so far recorded.

The Company is fortunate to possess a number of pieces of plate by contemporary British silversmiths. Three attractive wine cups, for the use of the Governor, Deputy Governor and most senior Past Governor, and made by Ian Calvert in 1990–6, were presented by David Rymer (Governor 1989–90). Each has a plain U-shaped bowl mounted on an irregularly twisted stem and is engraved with the Company's arms. Two further wine cups by Barry Whitmond, similarly engraved, were presented by members of the Kaye family in 2004–5 for the use of the Immediate Past Governor and the Principal Guest at Company feasts.

The Chapel has benefited greatly from a number of gifts of 21st-century silver. A striking altar cross and candlesticks in memory of Colin Shepherd

Top: Two-handled Porringer by George Gibson (York 1682).

Above left: Coconut Cup by William Busfield (York c1690).

Above: Venison dish by Robert Cattle and James Barber (York 1810).

Detail of the Altar Cross (2000).

Altar Cross and candlesticks by Christopher Philipson (London 2000).

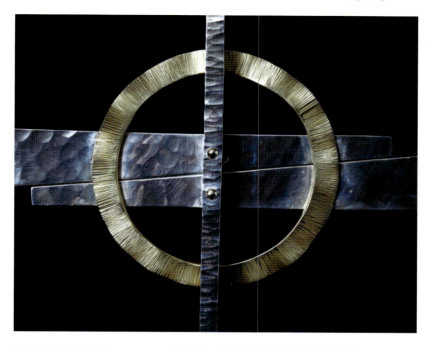

Right: *Charles I Wine Cup by Francis Bryce (York 1636–7).*

Far right: *Alms Dish by Christopher Philipson (London 2000).*

(Governor 1997–8) were commissioned by his family from the North Yorkshire silversmith Christopher Philipson. Designed to represent the timbers of the Hall, all three pieces are of hammered Britannia-standard silver, Millennium hallmarked.

Christopher Philipson again was commissioned by members of the Company to create an alms dish commemorating the millennium. The oval dish in the shape of the Company's seal has a sunken gilt centre etched with waves to depict merchants across the sea. The plain border carries the Company's crest and an inscription marking the millennium. The dish is similarly of Britannia standard.

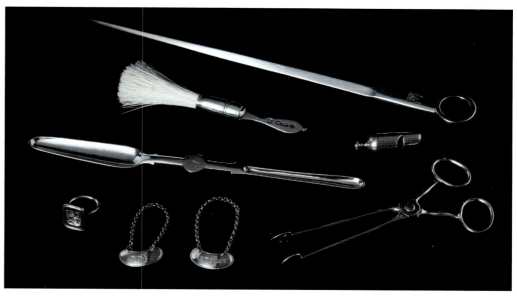

Barry Whitmond was the choice of Dick Reid (Governor 1993–4) and his wife to make a beautiful baptismal basin for the chapel. The circular dish has a wide border on which is engraved the Merchant Adventurers' Prayer. The hammered body of the basin has a raised centre which carries the London hallmarks for 2002.

The Company is also very fortunate to have on long-term loan from a member of the Company an interesting display of silver demonstrating the range of objects made by the York silversmiths in the three centuries between 1550 and 1850. Amongst the early pieces is a large 'pomegranate' peg tankard of 1654 by John Plummer. It carries lovely contemporary floral engraving, as does a fine porringer and lid (1676) by Thomas Mangy. Both show in their ornamentation the fine craftsmanship of these two famous York makers. Also of interest are two rare 'Death's Head' or funeral spoons. Engraved with a skull, and, on either side of the stem, 'Die to Live' and 'Live to Die', these 17th-century spoons were made for presentation to the family of a deceased member.

Amongst the later silver are no fewer than 25 examples of domestic objects made by the long-established (c.1770–1860) firm of Hampston & Prince, latterly trading under the Barber name. They demonstrate the sheer versatility of this distinguished provincial firm of silversmiths, making objects as diverse as a whistle, a shaving brush and labels for 'ketchup' and 'soy', these latter giving the lie to the commonly assumed modern introduction of these two sauces. Both collections of silver are on display at the Hall.

Opposite: *Wine cups by Ian Calvert (London 1990–6).*

Top: *'Death's Head' Spoons by Thomas Mangy (York 1665 and 1679).*

Top right: *Domestic objects (York 1770–1860).*

Above: *Baptismal bowl by Barry Whitmond (London 2002).*

Right: *The Company's collection of silver in the Governor's Parlour.*

List of Masters/Governors of the Mercers and Merchants of York from 1432

William Bedale	1432	John Harper	1482	John Thornton	1528
Richard Louth	1433	Thomas Scotton	1483	Robert Whitfield	1529–30
William Bedale	1434	John Hagge	1484	John Hogeson	1531–2
John Raghton	1435	John Gyllyot	1485–6	John Shawe	1533–5
Thomas Kirke	1436–41	Thomas Fynch	1487–8	Robert Hall	1536–8
John Catrike	1442	John Shawe	1489	John Shadloke	1539–41
Thomas Scauceby	1443	George Kirke	1490–1	Robert Paycok	1542–3
John Gudeale	1444	John Elwald	1492	Peter Robynson	1544–6
John Calton	1445–6	John Stokdall	1493	William Watson	1547–8
Thomas Crathorn	1447	Thomas Darby	1494–5	Thomas Appilyerde	1549–51
John Calton	1448	John Norman	1496	James Harryngton	1552–4
John Cateryk	1449–50	John Metcalfe	1497	William Beckwith	1555–6
Thomas Scauceby	1451–8	John Stokdale	1498	Ralph Hall	1557–9
John Gyllyot	1459–60	William Nelson	1499	George Hall	1560–2
Thomas Beverley	1461	John Gylliot	1500–1	Robert Paycoke	1563–5
Thomas Scawsebe	1462	Alan Staveley	1502–3	William Watson	1566–7
John Kent	1463	John Byrkhede	1504	Gregory Paycock	1568–71
Thomas Scawsebie	1464–5	John Stokdall	1505	Christopher Paycock	1572
John Ferriby	1466	Thomas Jameson	1506	Christopher Herbert	1573–5
Unknown	1467	John Lincoln	1507	Robert Brooke	1576–7
Robert Walkar	1468–70	Alan Staveley	1508	William Robynson	1578–80
Thomas Wrangwis	1471–2	John Shawe	1509–11	Thomas Appleyerd	1581–3
John Tong	1473	William Wright	1512–14	Ralph Richardson	1584–6
John Fereby	1474	John Norman	1515–16	Robert Brooke	1587–8
Richard Yorke	1475	Paul Gillor	1517–18	Thomas Mosley	1589
John Gyliot	1476	Thomas Burton	1519–20	William Robynson	1590–1
William Todd	1477–8	Thomas Rasyng	1521–2	Henry Hall	1592–4
Henry Williamson	1479	Peter Jackson	1523–5	Thomas Mosley	1595–7
William Brounflete	1480–1	Robert Wylde	1526–7	Thomas Herbert	1598–1600

George Rose	1601–3	Samuel Dawson	1722–5	Joseph Kimber	1847–53
Christopher Consett	1604	Henry Pawson	1726–7	Thomas Bell	1854–6
Robert Harrison	1605–7	William Dobson	1728–30	John Francis Taylor	1857–9
Thomas Mosley	1608–10	William Garforth	1731–2	John Manstead	1860–2
William Brearey	1611–13	James Dodsworth	1733–5	John Sampson	1863–5
Elias Micklethwaite	1614–16	Benjamin Barstow	1736–8	Lancelot Foster	1866–71
William Robinson	1617–19	George Barnett	1739	John Francis Taylor	1872–4
Matthew Topham	1620–2	William Hotham	1740–2	William Cowling	1875–7
Christopher Dickenson	1623–5	George Skelton	1743–5	Henry Foster	1878–80
Edmund Cowper	1626–8	Richard Lawson	1746–8	Joseph Terry	1881–2
Thomas Hoile	1629–31	Francis Jefferson	1749–51	Lancelot Foster	1883–4
William Breary	1632–4	Henry Grey	1752–4	T.P. Bulmer	1885–6
Henry Thomson	1635–7	Henry Myars	1755–7	Richard Dresser	1887–9
William Scotte	1638–40	John Wakefield	1758–60	W.H. Gainforth	1890–1
John Geldart	1641–2	Thomas Spooner	1761–3	Samuel Border	1892–4
Christopher Breary	1643–4	Thomas Barstow	1764–6	Edward Rooke	1895
John Geldert	1645	John Bradley	1767–9	J.B. Sampson	1896–8
Leonard Thomson	1646–8	Seth Agar	1770–2	J.J. Hunt	1899
Robert Horner	1649–51	John Stow	1773–5	Sir J. Sykes Rymer	1900–2
William Taylor	1652–4	Edward Smith	1776	John Cross	1903–4
Henry Thomson	1655–7	Thomas Bowes	1776	Arthur Jones	1905–6
George Lamplugh	1658–60	Hugh Robinson	1777–80	W.H. Waddington	1907–8
Bryan Dawson	1661–3	Thomas Spooner	1781–2	Lancelot Foster	1909–10
Christopher Topham	1664–6	Edward Stabler	1783–5	James Melrose	1911–12
Sir Henry Thomson	1667–72	Henry Myers	1786–8	Lancelot J. Foster	1913
Richard Metcalfe	1673–5	Thomas Smith	1789–94	George Crombie	1914–15
Yorke Horner	1676–8	John Hay	1795–7	H. Ernest Leetham	1916–19
Thomas Williamson	1679–81	George Gibson	1798–1800	J.B. Inglis	1920–1
Thomas Carter	1682–4	Emanuel Stabler	1801–3	Wilfred Forbes Home	
Philip Herbert	1685–8	George Peacock	1804–6	Thompson	1922
Sir Stephen Thompson	1689–90	Edward Prest	1807–9	Cecil Ben Johnson	1923
Andrew Perrott	1691–4	William Bilton	1810–12	Sir John J. Hunt	1924–5
Samuel Dawson	1695–7	George Healey	1813–15	Sir Francis Terry	1926
Sir Gilbert Metcalfe	1697	James Saunders	1816–18	Norman T. Crombie	1927
Andrew Perrott	1698–9	Robert Jefferson	1819–21	Sidney Leetham	1928
Samuel Dawson	1700	John Hodgson	1822–4	J.B. Morrell	1929
John Pecket	1701–5	Seth Agar	1825–7	Edwin J.L. Rymer	1930
Nathaniel Wilson	1706–7	Henry Stead	1828–31	William Dove	1931
Elias Pawson	1708–10	George Hanson	1832–4	Oscar F. Rowntree	1932
Charles Perrot	1711–13	John Jackson	1835–7	Gilbert Yorke Johnson	1933
John Welburn	1714–15	John Catton	1838–40	Reginald Hunt	1934
Richard Thompson	1715–18	John Lyth	1841–3	Noel G. Terry	1935–6
William Garforth	1719–21	Henry Bellerby	1844–6	John Triffitt	1937–8

Arnold S. Rowntree	1939	Percy G. Rodger	1964	George Peter Herbert	1988
H.H. Wilberforce	1940	The Right Hon. The Earl		David Sykes Rymer	1989
Edward Walker	1941	of Halifax	1965	Richard C. Wheway	1990
G.S. Hughes	1942	Mark Horsley	1966	Michael T. Barstow	1991
H.R. Hall	1943	Arthur D. Gladwin	1967	Roderick W. Oliver	1992
T.G. Leonard	1944	Charles W. Robinson	1968	Dick Reid	1993
Harold E. Bloor	1945	H. Brian Hall	1969	John L.C. Pratt	1994
Oliver Sheldon	1946	William Anelay	1970	John M. Raylor	1995
C.H. Cross	1947	W. Leslie Pratt	1971	H. Christopher S. Hall	1996
Arthur Sykes Rymer	1948	C. Wilfred Oliver	1972	Colin Shepherd	1997
G.N. Paul Crombie	1949	Claude C. Fairweather	1973	Ashley Burgess	1998
George Herbert	1950	Charles G. Wheway	1974	Lindsay Mackinlay	1999
H.L. Creer	1951	Sir Geoffrey Wrangham	1975	Michael Grills	2000
Christopher J. Rowntree	1952	Stephen W. Harland	1976	Trevor Copley	2001
W. Louis Lawton	1953	Richard E. Terry	1977	Darrell Buttery	2002
Geoffrey Thompson	1954	Lewis E. Waddilove	1978	Andrew Marr	2003
Bernard P. Johnson	1955	R.F.H. Stephenson	1979	Adrian Horsley	2004
Peter Rowntree	1956	Francis F. Johnson	1980	Nicholas McMahon Turner	2005
D.L.T. Creer	1957	J. Francis L. Robinson	1981	Peter Addyman	2006
J.G. Sykes	1958	J. Michael Saville	1982	David Ashton	2007
Peter N.L. Terry	1959	John Sykes Rymer	1983	Anthony Robards	2008
K.W.H. Bloor	1960	Sir Peter Shepherd	1984	Paul Shepherd	2009
John Saville	1961	Jack Penty Birch	1985	Richard Haynes	2010
C. Wilfred Robinson	1962	Stanley Howard Burton	1986	Nicholas Nightingale	2011
Ian F. Crombie	1963	Sir Donald Barron	1987		

The Company wishes to express its deep gratitude to the following for their generous support without which this book could not have been published:

The legacy of the late Michael Hollingbery
The Noel Terry Trust

Peter Anelay
David Ashton
Sir Donald Barron
David Barstow
James Barstow
Michael Barstow
Julian Bedford
Christopher Birch
David Blackburn
Rodger Booth
Trevor Copley
Genevieve Davies
Peter Davies
Steve Davis
Michael Dawson
Mark Deere
Edward Denison
Kenneth Dixon
Tony Faith
James Finlay
Michael Grills
Christopher Hall
Richard Haynes
Nicholas Hildyard

Adrian Hitchenor
Gordon Horsfield
John Horsley
Denise Howard
Holgate Illingworth
Ian Johnston
John Kinnell
Maureen Loffill
Peter Lyddon
John Machin
Lindsay Mackinlay
Richard Marriott
Martin Marsh
Tom Martin
David Mitchell Innes
John Morrell
Murray Naylor
Nicholas Nightingale
Christopher Oughtred
William Page
Tom Park
Andrew Pindar
John Pratt
Roger Raimes

John Raylor
David Rayner
Julian Richer
Carol Rymer
David Rymer
Tim Rymer
Michael Saville
Mark Sessions
Paul Shepherd
David Sheppard
Geoff Sherwin
Beverly Smalley
Alan Suggett
John Sykes
Richard Sykes
Richard Thompson
Rollo Thompson
The late Ron Thomson
Delma Tomlin
Ian Wand
Richard Wheway
Lesley Wild
Timothy Williams
Richard Wood

Index

Acknowledgements

The research and writing of this history of the Company of Merchant Adventurers of York took more than 18 months and the Company particularly wishes to acknowledge the dedication and commitment of members of the Editorial Working Group without whom this book could not have been produced. The Company is also very grateful to those others listed below whose contributions have included the writing of specific sections, significant research or invaluable advice.

The Editorial Working Group

Dr Peter Addyman*, Governor 2006–7

Darrell Buttery*, Governor 2002–3 and Honorary Curator of Paintings 1988–

Colonel James Finlay*, Clerk 1998–2010

Rita Freedman, Honorary Archivist 2008–

Dr Kate Giles, Department of Archaeology, University of York

Dr Pamela Hartshorne, Editor

Dr Jill Redford, Assistant Archivist 2002–

Michael Saville*, Governor 1982–3

Dr Richard Shephard*

Paul Shepherd*, Governor 2009–10 and Chairman of the Editorial Working Group

Others

David Blackburn*, Legal Advisor 1989–2000

Peter Brears, Food Historian

Gregor Grant*, Pensioners Co-ordinator

Richard Haynes*, Governor 2010–11

Lauren Marshall, Hall Manager 2009–

Nicholas Nightingale*, Governor 2011–12

Professor David Palliser, Honorary Archivist 2001–8

The Revd David Porter*, Honorary Chaplain 1992–2004

John Pratt*, Governor 1994–5 and Chairman of the Gardens sub-Committee 1998–

David Rayner*, Deputy Governor 2011–12

Dick Reid*, Governor 1993–4, Honorary Archivist 1975–88 and Honorary Curator Furniture and Treen 1988–

The Right Revd David Smith, Honorary Chaplain 2009–

Christopher Warner*, Honorary Curator Silver and Jewellery 1988–

Captain Stephen Upright RN, Clerk 2010–

Dr Katherine Webb, Borthwick Institute for Archives, University of York

Ivison Wheatley*, Clerk 1985–98

Dr Louise Wheatley, Honorary Archivist 1990–2000

Company Member

Picture credits

Images identified by page reference here are either copyright to or the property of the persons or institutions listed.

All efforts have been made to identify and acknowledge rights ownership of all content in this book. Should anyone have further information about rights or attribution, please contact Third Millennium directly.

All images, apart from those listed below, are reproduced with the permission of, and are copyright to, The Company of Merchant Adventurers of the City of York. The following images appear in alphabetical order and are copyrighted as follows:

Peter Addyman 85; **Nikki Bowling** 87BR; **Bridgeman Art Library** 13T, 28R ; **Bright White Ltd** 106; **Permission to reproduce documents in the custody of City of York Council Archives and Local History has been granted** 21; **By kind permission of the Dean and Chapter of York** 22, 26; **Stephen Drury** 129; **Alfred Gill** 82TL; **Dr John Kinnell** 36BL; **Mary Evans** 114; **Kippa Matthews** 4, 7, 18, 24, 27all, 28L, 29b, 46all, 49all, 50all, 53, 55, 56R, 64, 74-75, 79T, 86BR, 89BR, 91all, 92TR+M, 93, 94TR, 95all, 96all, 97, 98BL, 99, 104, 108all , 110, 111all, 117, 121, 123, 130–1, 151R, 155, 157B, 158T+TR, 160BL+BR, 161all, 162, 163, 164, 165TL,TR+M; **Gavin Mist Photography** 118; **Mumbai Cathedral** 44; **Jeremy Phillips** frontispiece, 6B, 8-9, 19, 20, 30, 36-7, 40-41, 43, 57, 58-59, 66B, 88B, 100-01, 102, 103, 109all, 112-113all, 115, 116, 119, 122, 124, 125B, 127L, 132–3, 156B, 157T, 158BL,M+BR, 159, 165BR; *The Press* 76Bb; **Dick Reid** 87BL, 127BR; **Science & Society Picture Library** 63; **Paul Shepherd** 23, 32, 88TL, 89BL, 125T; **The Stained Glass Trust** 38; **Topfoto** 60M; **Courtesy University of York** 80T, 81; **Upper Cut Productions** 80B; **YMA/Andrew Festing** 140B; **YMA/Bob Brumby** 140TL; **YMA/John Langdon** 140TR; **YMA/Noel Harry Leaver** 145; **YMA/Peter Mennim** 141; **York Archaeological Trust/Michael Andrews** 107B; **York Archaeological Trust/Simon Chew** 13R; **Courtesy of York Art Gallery of a print on display at the Mansion House, City of York Council** 12B

Front cover image: **Peter Mennim**
Reverse cover image: **Jeremy Philips**

The York Merchant Adventurers and their Hall
2011 © The Company of Merchant Adventurers of the City of York and Third Millennium Publishing Limited

First published in 2011 by Third Millennium Publishing Limited, a subsidiary of Third Millennium Information Limited.

2–5 Benjamin Street
London
United Kingdom
EC1M 5QL
www.tmiltd.com

ISBN: 978 1 906507 57 2 (hardback)
ISBN: 978 1 906507 58 9 (paperback)

British Library Cataloguing in Publication Data
A CIP catalogue record for this book is available from the British Library.

Edited by	Pamela Hartshorne
Design	Matthew Wilson
Production	Bonnie Murray
Reprographics	Studio Fasoli, Verona, Italy
Printing	Gorenjski Tisk, Slovenia

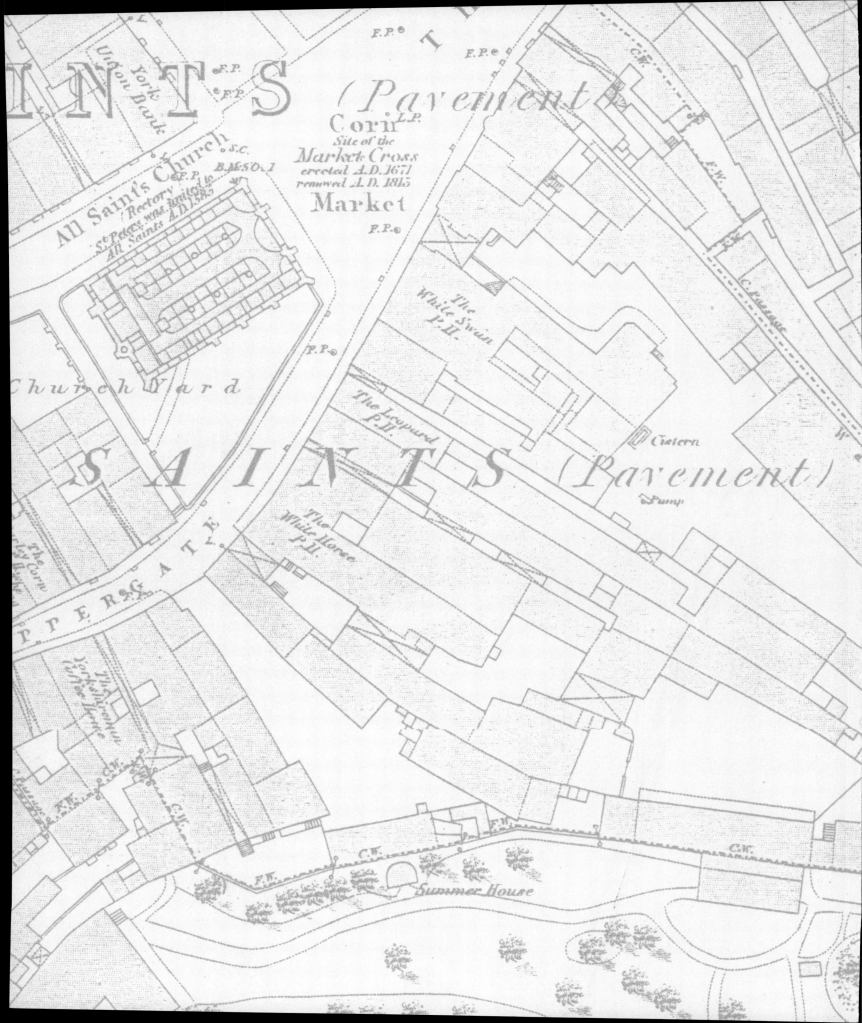

INTS (Pavement)

York Union Bank

All Saint's Church

Rectory

St. Peter's was united to All Saints A.D. 1585.

S.C.

B.M. 50.1

Corn

L.P.

Site of the Market Cross erected A.D. 1671 renewed A.D. 1815

Market

F.P.

F.P.

F.P.

F.P.

F.P.

F.P.

F.P.

F.P.

The White Swan P.H.

Church Yard

The Leopard P.H.

SAINTS (Pavement)

Cistern

Pump

The White Horse P.H.

The Corn

UPPERGATE

The White Horse

C.W.

C.W.

C.W.

C.W.

F.W.

F.W.

Summer House

C. Passage

F.W.